PUTIN

ON THE MARCH

— THE —

RUSSIAN

PRESIDENT'S

UNCHECKED

GLOBAL ADVANCE

DOUGLAS E. SCHOEN

Encounter Books

New York • London

First American edition published in 2017 by Encounter Books,
an activity of Encounter for Culture and Education, Inc.,
a nonprofit, tax exempt corporation.
Encounter Books website address: www.encounterbooks.com

Manufactured in the United States and printed on
acid-free paper. The paper used in this publication meets
the minimum requirements of ANSI/NISO Z39.48-1992
(R 1997) (*Permanence of Paper*).

FIRST AMERICAN EDITION

LIBRARY OF CONGRESS CATALOGING-IN-PUBLICATION
DATA IS AVAILABLE
ISBN: 978-1-59403-993-5
EBOOK: 978-1-59403-998-0

Interior page design and composition by BooksByBruce.com

Contents

Vladimir Putin Is Winning

How does a nation with a weak and vulnerable economy and inferior military go on an international military and intelligence winning streak the likes of which haven't been seen in years? How does a nation with a fraction of America's striking power exert its will in the Middle East and Eastern Europe and sow doubts about the legitimacy of American democracy—further polarizing and dividing an already-divided superpower?

How does Russia win?

—**DAVID FRENCH,** *NATIONAL REVIEW*[1]

[Russian information warfare is] about destabilizing democracy and pitting us against each other to limit the influence of the United States on the world stage.

—**JONATHON MORGAN, FORMER STATE DEPARTMENT OFFICIAL**[2]

Remember the 2012 presidential election, during which President Obama held off the challenge of the Republican nominee, Mitt Romney?

Remember the debates? There were three. In the first, Romney scored a decisive win over an off-his-game Obama. In the second, in the "town hall" format, the president rallied and had a good night. And in the third, devoted to foreign policy, the two candidates had this exchange:

OBAMA: Governor Romney, I'm glad that you recognize that Al Qaeda is a threat, because a few months ago when you were asked what's the biggest geopolitical threat facing America, you said Russia, not Al Qaeda; you said Russia—the 1980s, they're now calling to ask for their foreign policy back because, you know, the Cold War's been over for 20 years...

ROMNEY: Russia does continue to battle us in the U.N. time and
time again. I have clear eyes on this. I'm not going to wear rose-
colored glasses when it comes to Russia, or Mr. Putin.[3]

Obama won the soundbite war, and he won the election. But
five years later, it is clear that Romney's warnings were correct and
that Obama's dismissals of Vladimir Putin's Russia were woefully,
damagingly wrong.

Moreover, something else is clear: Putin and Russia are winning
at every level in which they are engaged, and there is little sign that
their victories will be reversed.

What has Putin achieved since that October evening when
Obama and Romney debated? Consider just the leading points: He
has forcibly annexed Crimea from Ukraine, causing international
condemnation for Russia but few other genuine costs; he has destabilized and weakened Ukraine, which is fighting a low-level war for
its independence and survival. And in the course of moving against
Kiev—in a part of the world Russia has always considered its "near
abroad"—Putin made a successful bet that the Western democracies, led by the United States, would do nothing to stop him. He was
correct then and he appears to be correct still.

In the charnel house that is Syria, again with the condemna-
tions of world leaders ringing in his ears, Putin boldly intervened
on behalf of Bashar al-Assad's dictatorship despite the risks of a
military confrontation with the United States or other Western
powers. Here, too, Putin bet that the United States and its Western
allies, when push came to shove, would want no part of any fighting
in Syria. They would talk, and they would levy sanctions, but if he
held firm and stood by his ally, he would prevail. And he has. Assad
is in power to stay, and Putin has made Russia a power broker in
the Middle East.

Putin's triumph in Syria has had the residual effect of causing a refugee crisis that is flooding Europe with desperate people,
most of them Muslim and more than enough of whom are prone

to radicalism and terror. European capitals are roiling with political anger and divisions over how to handle the influx of people—or whether to accept them at all. The rise of nationalist, antiglobalist parties in most EU countries can in many cases be closely tied to the Syrian refugee crisis, a crisis that likely wouldn't exist had Washington pushed back on Putin in Syria when it had the leverage to do so.

Indeed, a quailing Obama basically outsourced US Syria policy to Russia by declining to enforce his red line on chemical-weapons use; during Trump's presidential campaign, he eagerly followed suit, seeking to enlist Putin as some kind of regional policeman, especially on ISIS, to keep us out of Syria. This refusal to act is a serious abnegation of the US leadership role in the world, suggestive of a deep isolationism born of populist disgust with elite foreign policy after Iraq.

The refugee crisis and the Western paralysis and disagreement over Syria have fostered deep divisions and instability in the Western Alliance. An EU official, speaking on the condition of anonymity to Radio Free Europe/Radio Liberty, called it "Putin's year," and said that the Russian leader was "looking at a divided Europe"—just what he wants. The EU official was deeply concerned because the "United States for the first time is providing no counterbalance to [Putin]."[4] Indeed, the election of Donald Trump has tested the stability of the alliance. During the 2016 presidential campaign, Trump spoke critically of NATO and other traditional Western alliances, to the dismay of many; at one point, he even suggested that the durable postwar alliance was "obsolete."[5] (More recently, he retracted that judgment.) No previous presidential candidate had ever questioned the centrality of the Western Alliance. Trump is a patriot, but his skepticism—and, in my view, his naiveté—about the vital role of the Western Alliance plays into Putin's designs.

Under Putin, Russia forged a strong partnership with the Islamic Republic of Iran, just as Tehran was finalizing its nuclear deal with the United States—a deal almost entirely on terms that will benefit the mullahs, not Washington. Along with its Syrian achievements, Russia's new closeness with Iran makes it the new superpower of the Middle East. And just to make that point clearer, Putin has even reached out to Israel, which, after eight years of getting back-of-the-hand treatment from the Obama administration, was receptive to overtures from the Russian president.

Putin also continues to deepen his historic alliance with the People's Republic of China. What I have called the Russia-China Axis is the fundamental anti-Western, antidemocratic, anti-American force in the world today. And we remain ill equipped to deal with it, largely because we do not seem ready even to acknowledge its existence, its active moves around the world, and the implications it presents for our foreign policy.

Putin's victories have provided positive propaganda for his antidemocratic, anti-Western model of governance. With China and Iran as his partners, he is exemplifying a different model than the democratic, free-market framework, which has been reeling for more than a decade from the shocks of war, financial instability, inept leadership, and economic stagnation. Putin offers antidemocrats around the world new hope that there is another way to do things. His is a bleak and depressing model—but it is gaining ground, and not just in non-Western precincts. A portion of the right wing in Western democracies finds Putin's nationalist brio, social conservatism, and contempt for opposition appealing and even inspiring.

Finally, Putin is also having a huge impact right here at home in the United States—as everyone knows. As this manuscript goes to press, Congress and the Justice Department are still conducting investigations into the contacts between Russia and members of the Trump administration—with suggestions of potential collusion between the two during the 2016 presidential campaign. US intelligence agencies have confirmed that during the campaign, Russian hackers were responsible for the leak of thousands of e-mails from the Democratic National Committee. Russians were also identified as the source of "fake news" stories, such as the rumors about Hillary Clinton's health. The Russian role in the election was so prominent that it has set the always-warring political parties at each other's throats yet again, this time arguing over whether the process was legitimate or fatally compromised by the chicanery of an international foe. If it does nothing else, the Russian hacking scandal has succeeded in dramatically weakening Americans' already-shaky faith in our political system—but the story, of course, is far from over, and it might yet result in a full-blown, Watergate-level constitutional crisis.

Many believe that the United States is undergoing a period of discord and division not seen since at least the late 1960s; others, sounding more dire warnings, believe that the country is coming apart. A primary perpetrator in both critiques is Russia and the role of Russian influence. And this represents a Putin victory, too.

"President Trump talks about winning? Right now, Putin is winning," said former Homeland Security secretary Tom Ridge in March 2017. Ridge was talking about the investigations into Putin's election meddling happening in Washington. The goal for Putin, Ridge said, is "destabilization"—and he is achieving it. "Let's create chaos, let's create uncertainty, let's destabilize the political environment," Ridge said. "[The Russians] have done a wonderful job. If that was their goal, they have done it."[6]

It is indeed one of their goals, and has been for years. But it's only one front on the battlefield on which Putin operates.

A year ago, I coauthored a book with Evan Roth Smith called *Putin's Master Plan: To Destroy Europe, Divide NATO, and Restore Russian Power and Global Influence.* We wrote it as a warning to readers and, I hoped, to our political leaders that the Russian leader had a grand vision and a determined plan to execute it. Moreover, we warned, the plan was far from some abstract design: on the contrary, it was an active, ongoing reality, with some setbacks along the way but, for the most part, hard-earned, substantial successes. And we warned that the United States simply didn't have its eye on the ball in regard to Russia, and that, unless this changed, Putin would continue to gain.

Our warnings have been borne out. I'm hard-pressed to identify an important assertion that we got wrong. I say this not to boast but to underscore the gravity of the situation we face. The sobering truth is that Putin is meeting with sustained success in the three key areas in which he needs to prevail: foreign policy; control of Russian internal politics; and keeping the United States and our Western allies off balance, demoralized, and even destabilized.

* * *

Putin has done everything in his power to reclaim Russia's lost command of its traditional sphere of influence in Eastern Europe and its lost glory as a superpower. Those who dismiss what he has done as unsustainable, ill-advised, or reckless seem to willfully overlook one fundamental truth: he is getting away with it, and the more he is able to get away with and the longer he can do so, the stronger he becomes—especially as the Western democracies grow more fractured, both from their own internal problems and from the lack of a consensus on how to respond to him.

It is a fact that Putin has won in Syria. The West (and the Syrian people) has lost, in no small part because the countries refused to fight. Ceasefire talks don't even bother to include the United States or other Western powers. The game is over: Assad has prevailed because Putin was willing to put blood and treasure on the line to preserve his rule—and was willing to bet, wisely as it turns out, that the West would do nothing to stop him.

Putin, in Charles Krauthammer's words, left the Obama administration's presumptions in tatters. "The mantra out of this administration always was, 'You can't solve a civil war militarily,'" Krauthammer said. "The answer is, you can."[7] Indeed, Putin used force to achieve a clear objective: Save the Assad regime, and, as a collateral goal, discredit the West. He achieved both ends.

In December 2016, as the ceasefire was being negotiated without American participation, Moscow informed Washington that any US bombing strikes on Syrian targets without Russian approval would be met with force. The Russians put down a marker. They had a marker down from the beginning in Syria. They stand by their friends and allies. The Americans do not. Remember Hosni Mubarak in Egypt? President Obama let him be deposed—showing for all that the United States would stand by as an allied regime on which it had spent trillions twisted in the wind. Not Putin; when the chips were down and seemingly the whole world stood against Assad, and, by extension, Putin, the Russian leader did not waver. Four years later, he has won in Syria, pushed the United States out of any role in what happens next, and greatly strengthened the Russian hand. And all for an effort that wound up costing the Russians less in blood and treasure than Moscow had expected.

International observers agree that NATO stands today at its most unstable point since the alliance's inception. This is not all Putin's doing; Western democracies have grappled with political upheaval and institutional collapse for years. But a solid portion of it does have to do with Putin: Russian aggression has further divided Europe and undermined the stability of EU and the NATO alliance. The state of the EU today reflects in considerable degree the success that the Russian leader has had in eroding and dividing an alliance that he has always seen as a threat to Russian security and to his own neo-Soviet ambitions of renewed empire.

"The last thing Russia wants is a strong Europe," wrote Judy Dempsey for Carnegie Europe. "A strong Europe means having a coherent and united foreign, security and defense policy."[8]

Before he left office in January 2017, Bulgarian president Rosen Plevneliev warned about Putin. "The threat," he said, "is less about Russian tanks invading Europe and more about Russian influence dividing the Continent."[9] He said that his country was under attack by Russian hacking and propaganda during a referendum and local elections. He urged Western leaders to recognize that they were in a "dangerous and unpredictable" confrontation that he called "Cold Peacetime." He warned: "The game of Mr Putin is to make other countries dependent."[10]

But it was too late. Bulgaria had already elected a pro-Putin regime.

Donald Trump may prove to be a successful president, but, so far, his impact on the Western Alliance has been a destabilizing one—in no small part because of perceptions that he is sympathetic to, or at least apathetic about, Putin's designs. Our NATO and EU allies don't necessarily believe that the United States is on their side. This was made dramatically clear when the EU's "most senior Brexit negotiator," a member of the European parliament from Belgium, launched an attack on Trump and Putin, calling them a "ring of autocrats" who want to destroy Europe.[11]

"Not only do they like each other, they also have one thing in common," said Guy Verhofstadt. "Bashing and destroying our way of thinking, our values, our European liberal democracy."[12]

Putin has also taken Turkey out of the Western/NATO orbit, even if Ankara technically stays a member of the treaty organization. He turned Turkey away from the United States, all the while "winning" on Syria. Before recent years, this would have been thought of as an unfathomable development, and in fact it was unfathomable even more recently when Russia and Turkey came to loggerheads in Syria. During the Syrian conflict, Turkey, allied with the United States, worked furiously for the overthrow of Assad, Putin's client and the ally of Shiite Iran, the natural rival of and frequent meddler in Sunni Turkey. And Putin worked just as furiously to save Assad.

Russia's success in Syria was bad enough on its own—the entire situation has been a humanitarian and political disaster—but, worse, Russia and Turkey have now found common cause. Again, a Western political-leadership vacuum was crucial in doing so. Now, Putin and Erdogan, along with the mullahs in Iran, are the power brokers in the Syrian future, having taken responsibility for the Syrian cease-fire. Turkey's Recep Erdogan, whom President Obama called "an outstanding partner and an outstanding friend" of the United States in 2012, is edging closer and closer to an alliance with Putin. Russia and Turkey have even begun joint bombing missions against ISIS.[13]

Further, Putin and Erdogan are restarting the Turkish Stream natural-gas pipeline, a gas route that would bypass Russia's existing pipelines through Eastern Europe to bring Russian gas to Western markets. The idea is that Russia, if troubles with Ukraine deepen, will be able to continue its gas transactions with Western countries like Germany and Italy without worrying about supplies being disrupted through the Eastern pipelines. The new pipeline, in other words, will allow Russia to cut off gas supplies to nearby countries like Ukraine while not having to disrupt sales to countries like Italy or Austria.

Even the assassination in Ankara of Russia's Turkish ambassador hasn't stalled the two countries' rapprochement. "A crime has been committed and it was without doubt a provocation aimed at spoiling the normalisation of Russo-Turkish relations and spoiling the Syrian peace process which is being actively pushed by Russia, Turkey, Iran and others," said Putin in an address to the nation. "There can only be one response—stepping up the fight against terrorism. The bandits will feel this happening."[14]

Few Western observers seem to have absorbed the magnitude of the Turkish move toward Russia. Turkey had been long regarded as NATO's Eastern partner. If its drift toward Moscow proves enduring, it could alter the power dynamic between Western Europe and Russia for years to come—by further weakening NATO, strengthening the hand of autocrats, and lessening the influence of the West in the Muslim world.

Putin has also built a strong and stable yet misunderstood alliance with China. For years, I have warned about the impending Russia-China axis. If anything, things have only grown worse. The Russia-China reconciliation has expanded and accelerated to degrees even I would not have imagined.

"Over these last decades," Putin said in October 2016, "we have developed quite unique relations of trust and mutual support [with China]."[15] That is an understatement.

The two nations, once sworn enemies, have much in common—the common denominator is the desire to check and contain American power. Their trade interests, especially in energy, have both deepened in recent years, and they have each posed a distinct variation of an anti-Western, antidemocratic alternative model of power—models that, as the West flounders, gain ground internationally and even win hearts in democratic countries. Their militaries, once facing off across heavily fortified borders, have been increasing joint exercises, especially in 2015 when they put together huge naval exercises in the Eastern Mediterranean. And both are neck deep in rogue-state support and patronage, from the Middle East to the Far East to South America.

In late July 2017, North Korea test fired an intercontinental ballistic missile (ICBM) that experts concluded could have the range to hit Alaska, if not major US cities (yet). The missile test prompted a new round of high-tension rhetoric between Pyongyang and Washington, with President Trump warning Kim Jong-un that the North faced "fire and fury" if it continued to make threats.[16] Even more disturbingly, the tests seemed to represent a quantum leap forward for North Korea's missile-development efforts; most previous tests, while concerning, were usually marked by failure, sometimes abject failure, suggesting that the North was a long way from missile viability. But with this one, Pyongyang had attained a serious missile capability apparently overnight. How?

In early August 2017, an answer emerged, in the opening paragraph of a bombshell *New York Times* report: "North Korea's success in testing an intercontinental ballistic missile that appears able to reach the United States was made possible by black-market purchases of powerful rocket engines probably from a Ukrainian factory with historical ties to Russia's missile program, according to an expert analysis being published Monday and classified assessments by American intelligence agencies." The report went on to detail how US analysts had studied photos of Kim inspecting the new missiles' rocket motors and concluded that they derived from old Soviet designs. The motors are thought to be powerful enough that "a single missile could hurl 10 thermonuclear warheads between continents." The focal point of the activity is thought to be a missile factory in Dnipro, Ukraine, which in Cold War days made the deadliest missiles in the Soviet arsenal.[17]

The North Korea/Russia/Ukraine missile story has been the strongest sign yet of a phenomenon that remains largely unknown to the general public: the tightening embrace between Russia and North Korea. Putin first visited North Korea in 2000; his ties with Kim Jong-un's father, Kim Jong-il, were fairly strong, but most observers continue to associate the Hermit Kingdom with its traditional benefactor, China. Putin's Russia, however, is moving closer and closer to a newly meaningful alliance with Pyongyang. Multiple reports in April 2017 indicated that Russia was massing its troops along its border with the Hermit Kingdom in the aftermath of a tense stare-down between the United States, Pyongyang, and Beijing over one of North Korea's recent missile tests. Putin took no action against Kim when North Korea fired a ballistic missile in February 2017. He has even defended the North Korean nuclear program as one of self-defense. And now, with the Ukraine story, we have more insight into why he would take such a position. (A few weeks after the *Times* report on the Ukrainian factory ran, Russia flew nuclear bombers over the Korean Peninsula, flexing its muscles on the same day that the United States and South Korea were conducting military exercises.)

Russia has become North Korea's leading fuel supplier. Moscow and Pyongyang are finalizing a labor-and-immigration agreement. And North Korea's state-controlled news agency lists Russia as a top ally of the DPRK. (Putin even congratulated North Korea by sending "a friendly greeting to your country and your people on the occasion of the 71st anniversary of Korean liberation."[18])

Then, on September 3, 2017, North Korea detonated a powerful device underground that it claimed was a hydrogen bomb—and it further claimed that the bomb could be put on an ICBM that could reach the United States. The blast equaled the magnitude of a 6.3 earthquake. A few weeks later, the UN passed the harshest sanctions against Pyongyang yet—but those sanctions weren't nearly as strong as Washington wanted, because Russia, in tandem with China, had watered them down. Washington had previously sought a total ban on oil shipments to the North, but Russia and China killed that provision and forced the United States to settle for mere limits on the country's oil imports. Instead of a halt on all oil flowing into North Korea, the imports were capped at their current levels. Only after weakening the sanctions did Russia and China agree to vote for them. The United States was effectively blocked from taking stronger action. Teaming up at the UN is just one element of the deepening Russia-China partnership. Recent months have also seen greater security cooperation between the two countries. As they continue to find common ground against the United States, the two countries held their first joint naval drill in the South China Sea and both have condemned US plans to deploy a missile shield in South Korea. A Russian general said that their military was working with China to counter an expansion of US missile defenses.

Putin's support of Iran, meanwhile, shows no sign of lessening. Moscow continues to be a vital supplier of nuclear equipment and other weapons to Tehran. The Persian Gulf superpower continues to play a central role in Putin's global vision of controlling energy supplies, checking American influence, and building out Russia's regional and global reach. Putin has met with enormous success on all these goals in recent years, but has done so especially in his desire to become a Middle East power broker. The Syrian War has been one piece of the strategy; the Russia-Iran alliance has been another. A bloody and destabilized Middle East filled with ISIS-destroyed failed states and hemmed in by Russia and Iran to the north and east suits him fine. It leaves him in a similar position to that which Stalin found himself in at the end of World War II: as the grand military power bestriding a swath of "blood lands" (as a contemporary historian has described them). The Moscow-Tehran partnership has the added benefit of diminishing the influence and example of Sunni supremacists such as ISIS in the countries and regions of Russia's near east—for example, Chechnya.

Putin has also pushed back on President Trump's description of Iran as a terrorist state, lauding Tehran as a "good neighbor and reliable and stable partner."[19] And it must be, considering that, according to retired general Jack Keane, the Iranians are helping Moscow run arms to the Taliban in Afghanistan.[20] It's striking that Tehran would facilitate Russia's assistance of the Taliban—the Iranian regime is Shia, the Taliban, Sunni. But Russia and Iran share a common goal: to destabilize the United States and erode public support for its mission in Afghanistan. For that, the compromises are worth making.

* * *

At home, Putin has been relentless and purposeful in his fortification of Russian military power and tightening control on Russian civil liberties and the political process. He has upgraded his military and nuclear arsenal.

At a speech to his top military advisors, Putin declared that the Russian military "is ready to defeat any country that dares challenge it." He continued: "We can say with certainty: we are stronger now than any potential aggressor. Anyone."[21] That pointedly includes the United States. But Putin isn't satisfied. He has pushed his brass to "strengthen the strategic nuclear forces," believing that these forces "must be taken to a higher level of quality so that they are capable of neutralizing any military threats."[22] Specifically, he wants to fortify Russia's nuclear triad—that is, its nuclear weapons based on land, in submarines, and in long-range bombers. And he pushes for these measures with renewed confidence, since he was successful in negotiating deep reductions to the United States' nuclear arsenal—without corresponding cuts on Moscow's part.

It's not all strengthening arsenals and building stockpiles, either. Putin has begun moving these missiles into strategic areas, with recent reports suggesting that he has moved "nuclear-capable missiles close to Poland and Lithuania"—two countries in Russia's traditional sphere of influence that have embraced Westernism and that he hopes to destabilize. A Putin advisor warned that "impudent behavior" could have "nuclear consequences."[23]

While he strengthens his military hand, Putin tamps down

opposition in Russia, despite deep despair in the Russian Federation. March 2017 saw the biggest outbreak of protests in Russia in five years, with more than a hundred arrests and warnings given over loudspeakers urging demonstrators to "'think of the consequences' and disperse now."[24] The protesters were angry about corruption allegations involving the Russian prime minister. Russian opposition leader Alexei Navalny was jailed for fifteen days after the demonstrations.

The activism was notable because many in Russia have lost heart with political resistance, with a large portion of Putin opponents either demoralized or intimidated. Putin has pushed for new laws that make public assembly more difficult and he has tightened restrictions on speech on the Internet—especially when it's critical of the government—and political advocacy. Journalists who have reported critically about his rule wind up dead with alarming frequency. Putin also enacted laws cracking down on NGOs. The primary restriction is known as the "foreign agent law," and it requires NGOs that receive funding from outside Russia to register with the government as foreign agents and subject themselves to audits, with heavy fines imposed on those that don't comply.

At the moment, it is difficult to tell whether the reawakening of Russian discontent will pose a problem for Putin. He has acted in typically strong fashion to squelch it, but one must hold out at least the possibility that his success in controlling the electorate, as has been the case with most authoritarian leaders, has a finite shelf life—though that might still mean many more years of control to come.

* * *

Finally, Putin is achieving major victories in what are perhaps, for the West, the most disturbing areas of all: he is directly and indirectly destabilizing Western democracies and political culture, weakening Western alliances, and helping to hasten the collapse of institutional legitimacy in the West.

Let's face it: the claimed Russian "hacking" scandal regarding the 2016 presidential election has done major damage to American confidence in elections. The matter is still under investigation in Washington, but intelligence agencies are confident that the Russians were behind the hacking of computer systems of the Democratic National Committee as well as the private e-mail systems of Hillary Clinton and John Podesta. The e-mails were handed over to Wikileaks, which then released them online, to explosive effect. Evidence also suggests that Russian cyberwarriors are responsible for a host of fake-news stories during the 2016 election cycle, which may have influenced voters. A former Russia Today anchor, Liz Wahl, even admitted that the Russian media's "ultimate goal" was to "undermine democracy" and "faith in our institutions, like the media."[25]

It really doesn't matter whether you believe, as many Democrats do, that Putin and his fake-news propagators, along with the Wikileaks data dumps that only seemed to punish the Democrats, resulted in the election of Donald Trump or you believe, as most Republicans do, that these incidents played only a minimal role in the election results. As usual, we are missing the more fundamental issue: regardless of how much influence the Russian hacking had on the election result—if any—it speaks volumes about the porous nature of our electronic systems and about Russian capabilities to tap into them and shape US news gathering, reporting, and data management.

And that, in turn, leads to the real impact of Putin's electronic skullduggery: it has further exacerbated our political divisions and further eroded the American public's confidence in our institutions. Even before the hacking scandal broke out, that confidence was pretty low: A March 2016 Gallup poll found that only 30 percent of Americans thought that the election process was working well, with 66 percent considering the system "broken." Americans expressed majority support in just three institutions: the military, the police, and small businesses.[26]

Why should Putin care whether his hackers helped defeat Hillary or whether they had minimal impact? He has achieved something much more substantial: American political dissolution. If you create doubt in the minds of Americans that their voting systems and the heart of their democracy itself is up for grabs, it is irrelevant whether your efforts "changed the election" or just "influenced the election." What matters is that Americans, who had already lost confidence in their main political institutions, now have pretty much the same doubts about their election system.

In eroding American confidence in this way, Putin succeeds in putting Russia, with its corruption and notorious oligarchs, on the same footing with the United States. It helps him reinforce the message that he has been sending for years: Your system is just as corrupt as mine; stop preaching and clean up your own backyard. And now an American president is repeating that message. Trump has cynically shrugged off interviewers' questions about Putin's repression and the mysterious deaths that haunt the Russian political system by more or less asking: You don't think we kill people, too?[27]

Beyond the hacking scandal, Putin has been roiling American politics for years. Depending on changing political fortunes, our two political parties have sounded different messages about Russia: Under Obama, first it was reconciliation and then it was impasse; under the Republicans, first it was impasse, with Romney's warnings during the 2012 campaign, and more recently, under Trump, we've heard themes of reconciliation, or, at least, constructive engagement. This volatility points up how destabilizing of an influence Putin has been, and how Russia's international behavior has unmoored both parties from traditional judgments. Neither party has figured out how to think about the Russian challenge.

Finally, it has only recently dawned on Washington and its Western allies that Russia has devised and implemented a new form of information warfare that often includes fake news or conspiracy theories, and which is designed to undermine Western politicians and governments and spread Russian nationalist or other oppositional viewpoints. Whether doing it through news-and-commentary networks like Sputnik and RT or through social-media accounts, the Russians have become diabolically effective at undermining political stability and sowing the seeds of public dissension and upheaval by way of spreading disinformation about Western political leaders, governments, and news events. Whereas Cold War Russian propaganda often looked ponderous and obvious to Western eyes, the new Russian information warfare is highly effective, and it fools Westerners regularly—making it another key element in Putin's toolkit of provocation.

To take just one example among many, Russian operatives used Facebook to post bulletins calling citizens of an Idaho town to an urgent meeting to address the "huge upsurge of violence toward American citizens" by Muslim refugees recently settled there.[28] There was no such upsurge in violence; the bulletin was posted by a group called Secured Borders, which, it was eventually revealed, was a fake account created by a Kremlin-linked Russian company that regularly spreads fake news.

What is the point of all this information warfare? Former State Department official Jonathon Morgan summed it up best, pointing out that Russian aims are less about single specific goals—like influencing who wins a US presidential election—and more about making a broader, enduring impact: "This is more about destabilizing democracy and pitting us against each other to limit the influence of the United States on the world stage."[29]

* * *

A year ago, at the end of *Putin's Master Plan*, my coauthor and I concluded:

> The fundamental issue . . . is that the United States is not engaged. If the history of the last century has made anything clear, it is that failing to counteract the behavior of aggressive nations will only encourage more of the same. That is what we have seen here. The United States is simply absent. It is not that we are leading from behind; we are not leading at all . . . we have no clear policy, no strategy, and no plan.[30]

I would like nothing more than to be able to now write that—better late than never—the United States has grasped the magnitude of the Russian challenge and how much ground we have already lost to Putin. So far, however, the signs remain grim. Donald Trump remains blasé at best and dismissive at worst about the audacious and outrageous Russian interference in the 2016 election. It is remarkable to me, a lifelong observer of American politics, that an American president would be so unconcerned about this obvious attempt to compromise our electoral process. The attempt—regardless of its success—deserves nothing but absolute condemnation and resolute determination to prevent a repeat. But Trump has spent most of his presidency minimizing the seriousness of what Russia has done.

On the foreign policy front, the administration, as yet, seems incoherent in its response to Putin and Russia. Trump sent signals during the presidential campaign that he wanted a new kind of relationship with Putin, but as president he has flirted with confrontation—especially in April 2017, when the United States bombed Syrian positions after Assad unleashed gas on his own people. That action led to several days of high tensions, in an atmosphere that briefly reminded some of the Cold War. Was Trump's move a sign of a new and principled American posture on Russia or merely a one-shot? Time will tell.

In this brief follow-up to *Putin's Master Plan*, I want to bring the story up to date: by making clear that Putin remains very much on the march, that he wins much more often than he loses, and that he continues to pose a mortal threat to the Western Alliance. We are running out of time to wake up to the dangers he poses.

PART ONE

GOING OPERATIONAL

CHAPTER ONE

Russia's Ongoing Aggression

As we argued in *Putin's Master Plan*, Russia works relentlessly to undermine NATO, destabilize Europe and America, dominate the Middle East, and project its power around the globe, in a way that some argue makes it even more dangerous than the Soviet Union was during the Cold War. From Ukraine to Syria, from the Baltics to the Balkans, Putin presses forward aggressively in order to restore what he feels is Russia's rightful status as the superpower dominating Europe, Asia, and even further afield. Consider his moves in Syria, his continued menacing of Ukraine, his serial violations of the Intermediate-Range Nuclear Forces, or INF, Treaty, and even his brazen penetrations of American airspace and sea lanes in the Atlantic. Such provocations follow a concerted strategy, and all of them will worsen without a coherent, strategic American response.

There is little sign that what many now regard as a Putin victory in Ukraine will be reversed or even contained. In May 2017, Putin and German chancellor Angela Merkel met and pledged to push to finalize the Minsk accords—the 2015 deal stipulating ceasefire terms in Eastern Ukraine, which are still on the table but no closer to fruition. Talk is cheaper than ever. The fighting continues.

In January 2017, more than thirty died in a clash between the Ukrainian army and pro-Russia rebels in the town of Avdiivka. Ominously, both sides used weapons banned under the ceasefire terms. Both accused the other of instigating the violence. The Organisation for Security and Co-Operation in Europe called the fighting the heaviest in a year.

"The current escalation in Donbass is a clear indication of Russia's continued, blatant disregard of its commitments under the Minsk agreements with a view of preventing the stabilization of the situation," reads a statement from Ukraine's foreign ministry.[1] Plans were discussed for evacuating the sixteen thousand residents of Avdiivka, where electricity and other utilities had been knocked out.

The attack came as the new Trump administration was reportedly considering lifting economic sanctions against Russia imposed by President Obama. At the time of this writing, Congress has defied the president and moved to stiffen sanctions. As Ukraine's president, Petro Poroshenko, put it, "The shelling is massive. Who would dare talking about lifting the sanctions in such circumstances? What additional proof is needed to bring the aggressors to justice?"[2]

In Eastern Ukraine especially, the ravages of war are felt. "Hundreds of thousands of people are living under the perpetual threat of shelling, shooting, and land mines. Their access to basics like food, water, and electrical power has been dramatically curtailed," said Peter Maurer, president of the International Committee of the Red Cross.[3]

CNBC's Dina Gusovsky identified four key groups fighting in Ukraine on behalf of Putin's aims: "Pro-Russian Ukrainians," who had backed the former pro-Moscow president Viktor Yanukovych; "Mercenaries paid by Russian interests, including ethnic Chechens"; Russian separatists; and Russian special forces, which, according to her reporting, "are on the ground in Ukraine and have been for months."[4] Moscow denies these claims, but its past denials—about "little green men," for example—have been widely debunked by news reports and international observers.

There is no question that, over the last several years, Putin has moved decisively toward victory in Ukraine. In the Donbas region, for example, schools are now closely following Russian educational standards, commerce is carried out in rubles, and Putin recently issued a decree recognizing passports and other documents issued by the separatist governments in Luhansk and Donetsk—which, in March 2017, seized control of about forty Ukrainian companies.[5] Critics point out that the Ukraine struggle has become enormously costly to Putin, and this is true; but my sense here is, again, that we are measuring Putin's operations by conventional Western standards of self-interest. By Putin's reckoning, what he has gained and stands to gain is worth the cost.

That same kind of thinking guides Putin's brazen efforts in Syria—another pursuit that, years ago, he was told was futile, wasteful, and against his own national self-interest by American diplomats like Obama's secretary of state, John Kerry. He didn't listen, seeing a crucial opportunity in Syria to expand Russia's military presence beyond its own waters—indeed, the Russian maritime strategy for 2020 stresses the "need to reestablish a permanent Russian Navy presence in the Mediterranean."[6] Thanks to an October 2016 treaty deal between Moscow and Damascus, Russia also established its first permanent air base in the Middle East. Moscow boasted that the new air defenses would be able to fight off a US airstrike; its forces were authorized to "shoot to kill" in such a scenario. In July 2017, Putin signed an agreement with Syria ensuring that Russia can keep the air base operating in Syria for nearly a half-century.[7]

Despite ongoing deescalation talks—and his pledged support for deescalation—Putin is clearly engaged in bombing efforts against rebel-held areas in Syria. Russian warplanes have waged a bombing campaign against US-supported opposition groups in Syria, even as Moscow claims that its military campaign in the country has formally concluded. On the contrary: Evidence shows that the Russians are reengaging militarily in Syria. In October 2016, Russian and Syrian warplanes pummeled opposition forces in Aleppo for a solid month. Observers described the bombing as the most intense since the start of the conflict; it killed more than 440 civilians, including 90 children, according to the Syrian Observatory for Human Rights.[8]

As a result of the Aleppo bombing, Washington suspended its plans to coordinate with Russia on counterterrorism strikes in Syria. In response, Putin withdrew from an arms-control agreement that required both the United States and Russia to dispose of thirty-four tons of plutonium.

US-Russian relations grew worse still in April 2017, after Assad launched another chemical attack against his people, this time on the town of Kahn Shaykhun. To punish Assad for this barbaric violation of international standards, President Trump ordered a cruise-missile strike on the Shayrat Airbase, which had carried out the attacks. All told, US Navy ships in the Mediterranean fired fifty-nine Tomahawk cruise missiles. Furious, Russian prime minister Dmitry Medvedev accused the Trump administration of violating international law and attacking "the legitimate Syrian government" without UN approval. And he referred to America-Russia relations as "completely ruined."[9]

The April 2017 tensions carried the weight of recent history. It was Assad's 2013 chemical strike against Ghouta that prompted calls for President Obama to enforce his previously announced "red line" against the Syrian dictator should he resort to chemical-weapons use. When Obama backed down, Putin helped ease his decision by brokering a deal with Assad in which the Syrian president would agree to give up his chemical weapons and submit to internationally monitored inspections in return for an American promise not to attack. American officials believe that Putin hasn't enforced this agreement with Assad, and the Trump administration even accused Moscow of bearing some responsibility for the 2017 chemical attack, since Russian military personnel were present at the base.

Russian diplomacy furthers Assad's war by other means. Russia has used its UN veto power to block UN Security Council resolutions against Syria eight times. Most recently, on April 12, 2017—six days after Trump's cruise-missile strike—Russia blocked a resolution empowering international officials investigating Assad's latest chemical attack. The resolution had "an anti-Syrian slant," complained Russia's deputy ambassador, Vladimir Safronkov. To which UN ambassador Nikki Haley responded: "Stop covering for Assad."[10]

Putin isn't just covering for Assad. He is backing him openly and covertly, politically and militarily. Western efforts up to now, such as they have been, have proved ineffective in halting his efforts. The grisly Syrian conflict has shown Putin's steely nerves and determination to pursue his aims regardless of Western condemnation.

Putin is also escalating tensions in the Baltics and in the Balkans—lands that Russia has historically dominated in its sphere of influence, if not claimed as its territory outright. Russian forces have conducted exercises simulating a Baltic invasion in which nuclear weapons are used. A February 2016 RAND corporation paper warned that a Russian invasion of the Baltic States could reach the capitals of Latvia and Estonia in less than three days. In April 2017, Lithuania's intelligence service claimed that "Russia has developed the capability to launch an attack on the Baltic states with as little as 24 hours' notice."[11] Latvian officials say that Russia has amassed two hundred thousand troops on its border. And in a war game planned for autumn 2017, Putin will perhaps send one hundred thousand troops to Belarus's border with Lithuania and Poland.

The United States has sent Special Operations forces to the Baltics to train troops from Latvia, Lithuania, and Estonia.[12] "They're scared to death of Russia," said General Raymond T. Thomas, the head of the Pentagon's Special Operations Command. "They are very open about that. They're desperate for our leadership."[13] The Baltic countries are particularly worried about Russia's recent deployment of Iskander ballistic missiles—which have nuclear capability—in Kaliningrad, an enclave of Russian territory between Poland and the Baltics. The three Baltic nations are ramping up their defense spending; Latvia's and Lithuania's military budgets are the fastest growing in the world. Lithuania has reintroduced conscription and is building a wall on the border it shares with Russia.[14]

As for the Balkans: In June 2016, Putin's ruling party, United Russia, signed an agreement with anti-NATO parties in Serbia, Montenegro, Bosnia and Herzegovina, Macedonia, and Bulgaria for the "creation of a militarily neutral territory in the Balkans" that would "form a territory of neutral sovereign states" made up

of these countries. "This project aims to become a regional strategic doctrine and in the future be incorporated into pan-European
considerations of a new continental security architecture," United
Russia said.[15] Lest this sound merely ceremonial, consider that,
according to the *Economist*, 64 percent of Serbs see NATO as a
threat. Or that Montenegro's government endured an October 2016
coup attempt in which it arrested twenty Serbian suspects, and
the prosecutor blamed Russian "state organs" for masterminding
the coup to prevent the country from entering NATO. Moscow,
of course, denied it.

* * *

A key part of what makes Russia so effective is hybrid war, which
the US Army defined as "the diverse and dynamic combination of
regular forces, irregular forces, and/or criminal elements all unified to achieve mutually benefiting effects."[16] In the case of Russia,
the toolbox has included cyberwarfare, propaganda and fake news,
economic threats, and destabilizing operations ranging from the
exacerbation of ethnic and nationalist strife to the use of "little green
men"—Russian army forces dressed without identifying insignia—
to initiate or support insurgent campaigns against the governments
of Russia's neighbors. In a January 2013 speech, Russian armed-
forces chief of staff Valery Gerasimov called for a "new kind of war"
that would be waged with "nonmilitary methods to achieve political
and strategic goals."[17] That same year, in a Russian military journal,
Gerasimov laid out the Gerasimov Doctrine, calling for asymmetric
war in which the Russian use of nonmilitary measures would outweigh military measures by a 4:1 ratio. That equation, along with the
element of surprise, proved crucial to Russian success in Crimea.

The Russian strategy is steeped in the use of propaganda and
disinformation, focused on winning the battle not only in the streets
but also in the television studios, the newspapers, and the hearts of
the people. Covering up his own actions is the purpose for Putin's
frequent accusations that the United States and NATO are engaged
in the very thing he is in fact doing—trying to take over a sovereign

nation—and why Gerasimov pointed out that the United States had practiced hybrid-war tactics for years. The goal of this "big lie" is to destabilize the enemy not just in the field but also in the media and in the chess match of strategy.

In April 2015, Anders Fogh Rasmussen, former NATO secretary general, warned that Russia was engaging in a "hybrid war" with Europe, working to undermine states from within. "Russia has adopted this approach and it is a mix of very well-known conventional warfare and new, more sophisticated propaganda and disinformation campaigns," Rasmussen said. The diplomat went on to say that Russia's current posture and tactics actually made the country more dangerous than the Soviet Union had been during the Cold War. "Even during the Soviet time they were hesitant to talk about nuclear conflict," he said. "Now we see an open debate. In that respect the Russia of today is more dangerous than the Soviet Union. The USSR was more predictable."[18]

If hybrid war is an asymmetric version of conventional war, Putin's aims in Ukraine can also be seen as an asymmetric version of his conflict with the West. Russia still lacks military superiority compared with the United States, but hybrid war—especially when combined with the audacity of the man waging it—evens things up.

Hybrid war is so flexible, in fact, that it can put conventional weapons to unconventional uses. Consider how Putin has used the S-300 missile to menace Georgia and other neighbors, as he has been doing for years. Putin has either positioned or has the capacity to position S-300s in Abkhazia and South Ossetia, the two Russian-occupied breakaway regions in Georgia. The Russians have the capability, a Georgian newspaper declared, of "inflicting paralyzing damage to Georgia's territorial integrity."[19] That kind of power means that Russia has de facto control over Georgian airspace, even if that control is exercised without a military demonstration. Putin can also potentially menace the airspace of the Baltic nations, none of which have fighter jets or effective air defenses. In Kaliningrad, just south of the Baltic region, Putin has stationed S-400 missiles, an even-more-advanced version of the S-300.

What matters most about hybrid war is less what specific tactics Putin uses than how the tactics fit into Russia's broader strategic vision. Putin has made it clear that he doesn't think that the United States or NATO is willing to confront him—perhaps even if he menaces a NATO country. Article 5 of the NATO treaty guarantees that an attack on one NATO member is an attack on all, but it says nothing about "air sovereignty." If Putin were to establish air dominance over a NATO nation, would his actions trigger Article 5—or would NATO members find a way to reason themselves out of it? These are the kinds of questions that Putin is forcing the West to ask itself.

Similarly, what if the Little Green Men show up in the Baltic states of Estonia or Latvia, both of which have sizable ethnic Russian populations? We've already seen how Putin has used (often bogus) complaints about the mistreatment of ethnic Russians to work his will in Crimea. What if the Little Green Men seized assets on the ground, under the guise of protecting ethnic Russians? The same question applies here as to the airspace violations: how will NATO regard these actions, and how will the alliance respond?

Hybrid war is an effective channel of the larger war that Putin is waging against the West on every front—political, military, economic, and ideological. Putin doesn't need a war to achieve his objectives—all he needs is the the consistent application of pressure, confrontation, and high-stakes moves to intimidate Washington and Europe into backing down. And Western dismissals of Russian capabilities don't account for the sophistication of Putin's tactics. "It is the allegedly backwards Russians who have adapted their war-fighting capabilities to the future," James Kirchick wrote, "and the supposedly advanced Westerners who have been caught in their dust."[20]

* * *

Aggressive and provocative moves by Moscow take on an even darker meaning, too, when considered in the context of the now-endangered Intermediate-Range Nuclear Forces (INF) Treaty, signed in 1987 by President Ronald Reagan and Communist Party general secretary Mikhail Gorbachev of the Soviet Union. In March 2017, General Paul Selva, vice chairman of the Joint Chiefs of Staff, told Congress that Russia had deployed a cruise missile in violation of the treaty. The deployment, Selva said, "violates the spirit and intent" of the INF Treaty and presents "a risk to most of our facilities in Europe." Moreover, the general said, "we believe that the Russians have deliberately deployed it in order to pose a threat to NATO and to facilities within the NATO area of responsibility."[21] It is the same cruise-missile system that the Obama administration objected to in 2014, when it was still being tested, warning that it was in violation of the INF accord.

Putin has long hinted at getting back into the game on cruise missiles. He has long questioned the INF accord, saying that the Soviet Union's decision to enter into it was "debatable to say the least." And he has complained that "nearly all of our neighbors are developing these kinds of weapons systems."[22] Now Russia is, too.

In the last several years, a number of other Russian cruise missiles have been suspected of potentially violating the INF Treaty as well. The conclusion depends in many cases on whether the missiles in question use an Iskander launcher, which has a range of several thousand kilometers. If these missiles—including the Kalibr and the Bastion—use Iskander launchers, they violate the treaty.

The biggest threat is to NATO. In his testimony to Congress, Selva voiced skepticism that the United States had many options that could force the Russians back into compliance, arguing that Moscow isn't terribly interested in conforming with the accord. Former NATO commander General Philip M. Breedlove, however, sees the Russian violation as being so serious that he has stated that it "can't go unanswered."[23]

The United States has endured yet another brand of Russian provocation: Russian planes' "buzzing" of American ships and a Russian submarine penetration in the Atlantic, right up to the edge of the international-waters borderline. In February 2017, a Russian Sukhoi Su-24 plane, flying at faster than five hundred knots, came within two hundred yards of the USS *Porter* in the Black Sea. This was preceded by another incident where two other Russian Su-24s came within three hundred yards of the ship, and a Russian Ilyushin IL-38 flew at an exceptionally low altitude. All four Russian planes had their transponders turned off, indicating that the Russians weren't interested in communicating with the Americans—a reckless move that risked grave consequences.

In April, the United States scrambled two fighter jets to intercept Russian bombers that were flying near the coast of Alaska, breaching what is known as the Alaskan Air Defense Identification Zone. US planes were sent out to intercept them, without incident.

Earlier, in February and March 2017, a Russian spy submarine, the *Viktor Leonov*, patrolled the Atlantic along the eastern US seaboard, coming within seventeen miles of the US mainland—although still technically in international waters. The *Leonov*, according to a CBS News report, is "built for spying," with sophisticated reconnaissance capabilities and equipment for intercepting communications signals.[24] While Russian ships have conducted such missions in the past, the sheer number of them conducted of late, and the brazenness of Russian pilots, clearly suggests that Russia is willing, at the least, to rattle US nerves—if not actually provoke a reaction.

CHAPTER TWO

Russia's Petro-Politics

In May 2017, a story broke revealing that Syria, in an effort to skirt international sanctions, had developed a secret deal with Venezuela to transport Syrian oil through Russia to the Caribbean. The plan involved selling the oil to Venezuela at steep discounts— just what the struggling, cash-poor socialist country needed, and just the kind of economic boon that Bashar al-Assad would prize as he struggled to hold onto power. Assad would be out of power today without the ministrations of Vladimir Putin; and with this news story coming out of the Caribbean, of all places, emerged the details of just how far Putin could extend his reach—in this case, to help not one but two pariah states, half a world away from each other.

It is no accident that when Russia extends its influence, or attempts to do so, the tools it commonly uses involve energy—a world market in which Moscow is a primary player. Russia has historically enjoyed the power and influence that accompanies a near monopoly on European gas imports, with its state-owned Gazprom already supplying one-third of European gas demand.[1] Russian energy influence extends to the Middle East and North Africa, too, where Putin is looking to use Russia's state-owned energy companies to get in on the action of Arab nations rich in fossil fuels.[2]

For years now, critics of the American disengagement from the Middle East, especially in Syria, have warned that US passivity would open doors for Putin to extend his influence not just politically but economically. Those warnings are becoming reality.

Rosneft, Russia's massive state-owned oil firm run by a close Putin associate, has been busy establishing itself in Iraq and Libya. In February 2017, Rosneft announced an agreement to buy crude oil from Libya's National Oil Corporation and to extend oil exploration in that country. It also announced that it would buy oil from Iraq's Kurdish region and help the Kurds find new markets for their oil. It was a big step for Russia's strategic move into the Middle East energy markets, a move made possible in part by the foothold provided by Putin's political and military strengthening of Bashar al-Assad.

The Kurdish deal is especially shrewd, showing Putin's geopolitical strategic vision. Russia is effectively telling the Kurds that it will take care of distributing their oil, which has been a problem for Erbil for years because of tensions with Baghdad over oil contracts. For the Kurds, letting Moscow handle distribution ensures that their oil will flow freely, bypassing Iraqi strictures. By doing so, Putin diminishes the power and sovereignty of a fragile government closely allied with Washington.

Russia has asserted its might in the Middle Eastern oil market for some time. In December 2016, Rosneft bought 30 percent of Egypt's offshore Zohr gas field. In February 2017, the same month that the firm announced its Libyan and Kurdish deals, it also announced that it would begin drilling in the Block 12 oil field in southern Iraq. The following month, Rosneft bought Egyptian crude oil for the first time and also signed a deal to supply the North African nation with liquefied natural gas (LNG). And Rosneft is also considering making a bid for offshore rights in Lebanon.

This is a dizzying litany of activity, much of it unprecedented. The new Russian deals "combine potentially good economics for Rosneft and good politics for the Kremlin," said Chris Weafer, a Russian investment strategist. "Expect more deals from Rosneft in the Middle East and North Africa and across the developing world."[3]

These moves are changing the balance of power in the Middle East, but Putin has been busy elsewhere, too—including in Europe. A key plank in his European strategy is Nord Stream 2, the new export-gas pipeline running from Russia to Europe and across the Baltic Sea, with a capacity of transmitting fifty-five billion cubic meters of gas per year. It represents the third and fourth lines of the gas pipeline Nord Stream; the first two were laid in 2011 and 2012. Russia plans to finalize Nord Stream 2 in 2019.

"The new pipeline, similar to the one in operation, will establish a direct link between Gazprom and the European consumers," the company said. What Russia is promising with Nord Stream 2 is a steady and reliable supply of Russian gas to Europe—highly desirable for Europeans, as the Russian company sees it, given that the continent's gas production is waning, even as demand grows.[4]

Nord Stream 2 will make Germany the main hub for gas imports into Europe—and allow the Russians to pump gas via a pipeline that bypasses Ukraine. The EU and the United States (at least under the Obama administration) long resisted this arrangement, concerned about the economic and political damage to Ukraine.[5] Eastern European countries like Slovakia and Poland also worry about the new pipeline strengthening Russia's leverage, especially given Moscow's past habits of restricting gas flows to its neighbors with whom they were engaged in political disputes—as it has done to Ukraine, Georgia, Moldova, and Belarus. Putin dismisses these concerns, calling the pipeline an "absolutely natural project" and "purely commercial" in nature.[6]

Nord Stream has Putin's characteristic approach written all over it. In Stockholm, Swedish political leaders oppose the pipeline, but in the tiny town of Karlshamn, local Swedes allowed a Gazprom subcontractor to store pipes for the project. Swedish national leaders view Nord Stream not only through an EU lens but also with concerns that come from being a northern neighbor of Moscow: They see the new Russian pipeline in the context of Putin's threatening moves in the Baltics.[7] Swedish defense minister Peter Hultqvist said, "We are against Nord Stream 2," calling it "a problem from a European perspective."[8]

As for the broader EU, it has expressed its objection to the pipeline as well, seeing it as an obstacle to EU goals to "diversify and secure gas-supply sources, curb dependence on major providers like Gazprom, and prevent a concentration of transit routes."[9] But the EU concedes that it has no legal authority to stop it from being built.

Nord Stream 2 is almost certain to become a flashpoint between Moscow and the EU—and it won't be the only one related to energy politics. Gazprom is moving boldly in its efforts to transport more gas to Europe: It has announced its intention to make use of the Trans Adriatic Pipeline, a key route on what is known as the Southern Gas Corridor. According to the TAP's official website, the SGC refers to "planned infrastructure projects aimed at improving the security and diversity of the EU's energy supply by bringing natural gas from the Caspian region to Europe."[10]

The TAP is vital to Europe because it would be the first non-Russian gas pipeline to the continent for almost a decade. Through the TAP, Europe could begin to lessen its dependence on Gazprom, which now captures a third of the European gas market.[11] It's one of the EU's highest priorities in this regard, and American investment has been involved, too. The plan up to now has been to bring Azerbaijani gas to Europe via the TAP. But Russian entry onto the scene will complicate this goal and potentially change the game. As one EU official put it, a Russian presence would be "totally contrary to everything we have agreed with partners."[12]

Taken together, Nord Stream 2, the incursions into the TAP, and the audacious and successful moves into Middle Eastern markets show a Russia determined to play its energy hand with all the power and savvy that it can muster.

CHAPTER THREE

Forming the New Russian Empire

Putin has pursued his vision of a reconstituted Russian empire with efforts to expand, deepen, and secure Russia's economic and political penetration of the former Soviet republics of Central Asia. In 2015, he scored a big victory in that regard with the creation of the Eurasian Economic Union (EEU), an organization with a reach of 183 million people and a GDP of $4 trillion. Russian efforts to dominate Central Asia have been only partially successful, however, given the economic adversity and political cross currents that roil the region. Putin does not allow temporary reversals to deter him from his objectives, though. He has shown that he can weather hardships and uncertainties and turn them to his advantage. The lack of any coherent US policy toward the region helps him in this regard. In the meantime, Putin has extended his drive for empire westward into Europe as well as southward into Central Asia.

In the process, he has successfully insinuated Russian influence and power into his western neighbor, Belarus, another former Soviet republic where many have begun to fear that they might be next on Putin's target list for takeover.

* * *

In late February 2017, Putin traveled to Kazakhstan, Tajikistan, and Kyrgyzstan, looking to solidify ties and work out pressing issues. The trip's success was generally regarded as a mixed success, but it did shed light on the state of relations between Russia and its Central Asian neighbors, all of which represent important elements in Putin's grand strategy. Central Asia bursts with oil and natural gas begging for export; Russian dominion would hand over to Putin some of the world's largest natural-gas fields and an energy market vital to both European and booming East Asian economies. These countries may be among the poorest in the world, but their vast reserves of natural resources make them strategically priceless. Beyond oil and gas, there is coal, uranium, gold, iron ore, and manganese. If Putin can consolidate control over Central Asia, it will help him fund military expenditures and secure the Kremlin's position astride strategic trade routes from Europe to Asia.

With this goal in mind, Putin launched the Eurasian Economic Union in 2015, consisting of Russia, Kazakhstan, Belarus, Armenia, and, most recently, Kyrgyzstan. He'd like to add Tajikistan to that mix, but so far, the country has demurred. Putin envisioned the EEU as his answer to the European Union and had taken earlier steps in this direction—forming the Customs Union of 2010 and the Common Economic Space in 2012.

The challenge for Putin is that by the time the EEU formally emerged in 2015, the economic and political landscape had changed considerably. The Russian annexation of Crimea in 2014 made many EEU member nations wary about the scope of Putin's goals and about the nature of his intentions toward the EEU. In Kazakhstan, for example, home to 3.5 million ethnic Russians, views on Ukraine have been divided starkly along ethnic lines. Ethnic Russians support Putin's move into the country; native Kazakhs tend to oppose it. And rather than seeing the EEU purely as an economic partnership, as Putin had pitched it, Kazakhstan and others began to sense that it was more of a political entity—and that Putin really intended to use it as an instrument of coercion. An early sign of that coercion came in 2013, before the EEU's formalization, when Moscow forced Armenia to reject the association agreement with the EU, thus keeping a nation that the Russians deem firmly within their geopolitical sphere cut off from potential Western suitors.

Moreover, given Russia's economic preeminence among the group of countries, the EEU could be more useful for Russia as a bilateral instrument than it has so far proven to be if it were to serve as a benefit for its member nations. Further, the union has deepened its dependence on Moscow. And even more so, the EEU merely serves as an instrument to promote the preservation of Russian language and culture; Russian is the sole official language of the organization.

In addition, global economic developments, like the plunge in the price of oil, weakened Putin's hand with his EEU allies. Overall, the EEU partners see many reasons not to trust Moscow.

Still, there is no question that Eurasian integration was "the common theme in Putin's tour of Central Asia," as Central Asia analyst Camilla Hagelund put it.[1]

In Kazakhstan, Putin sought to reach out to President Nursultan Nazarbayev, who has lately been sending signals that he would welcome economic assistance from the West (namely the EU) and from China. In response, Putin dangled promises of billions in economic investment. In Tajikistan, despite rumors of the country joining the EEU, Putin and President Emomali Rahmon did not even discuss the possibility. However, while there is no sign that it will join the EEU anytime soon, Tajikistan did agree to an expansion of the Russian military presence in the country, allowing Moscow to rent its Ayni Air Base, a significant win for Putin. (Tajikistan already hosts Russia's largest military base outside its borders, the 201st military base.)

And in Kyrgyzstan, Putin met with President Almazbek Atambayev, who will be stepping down from power near the end of this year as mandated by the country's constitution. Much speculation surrounds what role, if any, Moscow will play here, because a

Russia-friendly successor is crucial to Putin's designs. Veteran Putin watchers might have smiled wryly at his disclaimer: "As for internal political processes, they are not our business and we never interfere in internal processes of other countries, let alone our allies."[2]

The question about succession does not pertain to Kyrgyzstan alone. Kazakhstan's Nazarbayev is seventy-six years old and, by some accounts, has begun transferring more power to his parliament. It seems clear that Moscow will want to play a role in determining who the successor will be there, too.

Overall, what Russia is trying to do here, in the words of Lilit Gevorgyan, an analyst at the IHS Markit think tank, is to lock "as many countries as possible in tightly integrated Russian led economic, political and military blocs." Gevorgyan sees what Putin has achieved on this front as having more to do with the United States' abandonment of engagement with the area than with the strength of Russian initiatives—and, given the American absence, he sees the real obstacle to Putin's goal of strategic integration as coming not from the United States but from China.[3]

* * *

Meanwhile, the Crimean crisis worked against Russia in regard to Turkmenistan and Azerbaijan. The two countries, earlier at odds over control of the Caspian oil fields, found common cause in 2014 when they announced plans for a Turkmen-Azerbaijani pipeline to bring gas to Western markets. "The so-called Southern Corridor would bypass both Russia, Europe's major gas supplier, and Ukraine, the main route for existing pipelines carrying the fuel west," wrote Darren Goode of *Politico*. As he pointed out, at the moment, "Azerbaijan maintains that its pipeline is the only shovel-ready means of giving Europe an alternative supply in the next few years."[4] The pipeline could be finished in 2018 at the earliest. As I noted in chapter 2, the Russians have however responded with Gazprom announcing a bid to transport Russian gas via the Southern Corridor, thus defeating, if Moscow is successful, the very purpose of the Turkmen-Azerbaijani pipeline: the diversification and independence from Russian sources.

Putin has also made inroads with Uzbekistan, where Islam Karimov, president of the country since its independence and a strong nationalist, had long staunchly opposed Russian imperialism. In March 2016, Russia pardoned 95 percent of Uzbekistan's outstanding debt to Moscow. Writing for the *Diplomat*, Samuel Ramani saw Putin's debt forgiveness as a bold move that would "contribute greatly to bolstering Russian leverage over Central Asia." It would give Russia a stronger economic hand in the region to play against China, and it would help strengthen the already-considerable mutual security interests that the two countries share.[5] As if to prove that hypothesis, Shavkat Mirziyoyev, who succeeded Karimov after the latter's death in September 2016, has signed investment deals with Putin worth $12 billion and trade contracts worth $3.8 billion. "It is no exaggeration to say that we see this meeting as a new step in developing and strengthening the strategic partnership and alliance between our countries," he said. "We consider Russia a great power" that "plays a key part on the international stage."[6]

After some years spent developing stronger ties with the European Union and its pro-Western neighbor, Romania, Moldova also recently made a strong reversal in turning toward Moscow. President Igor Dodon, elected in December 2016, said that he wants to abandon the EU treaty in favor of the Russian-led bloc, the Eurasian Economic Union. Speaking of an EU free-trade agreement that he signed in 2014, Dodon said, "We have lost the Russian market and, strangely enough, our exports to the EU have also fallen. In other words, we have received nothing from signing the agreement." He called for a new "strategic partnership with Russia."[7] Score another one for Putin.

In Eurasia, Armenia has been a useful tool for Putin to expand his military presence. After being forced by Moscow to stay out of the European Union in 2013, Armenia seems to have embraced its Russian host. It became a full member of the Eurasian Economic

Union in January 2015, and, since then, Armenia has become increasingly involved with Russian defenses. In 2017, Armenian president Serzh Sargsyan announced the creation of a joint military-industrial complex with Russia in the city of Gyumri, suggesting a deepening of his country's military alliance with Moscow.

There are even signs, remarkably enough, that Georgia is tilting toward Moscow. Ostensibly, Georgia aligns itself with the EU. In June 2014, the country entered into an association agreement with the EU that opened it up to free trade with the union and closer ties with NATO. But more recently, the combination of economic shocks and benefits from Russian trade—which many see as a boon to the nation's agricultural sector—have pushed popular sentiment in Georgia toward the EEU.

* * *

Perhaps the nation most at risk of domination by Russia in the region is Belarus—the most closely linked to Russia of all post-Soviet nations. Since 1994, Belarus has been ruled by Alexander Lukashenko, who once defended his autocratic, totalitarian regime by declaring that it is "better to be a dictator than gay."[8] Lukashenko has long been a close and reliable ally of Moscow, and he serves as the president of a mostly imaginary entity known as the Union State of Russia and Belarus, envisioned as a commercial, military, and currency partnership. For Putin, keeping Belarus in the Russian sphere of influence is a necessary step on the journey toward Russian regional hegemony. Like Ukraine, Belarus was part of the Russian Empire and Soviet Union, and its history is inextricably linked to Russia's. Russian is spoken more widely in the country than Belarusian, and even Lukashenko usually speaks in Russian. Putin has always been staunch in his resistance to any efforts on Belarus's part to chart an independent course. As I and my coauthor, Evan Roth Smith, wrote in *Putin's Master Plan*: "Moscow will steadily exert more control over Belarussian affairs, likely through the Eurasian Economic Union, until Belarus becomes indistinguishable from a province of the Russian Empire—as it once was."[9]

In Belarus as elsewhere, however, Russia's annexation of Crimea changed the dynamics. Lukashenko, feeling threatened, refused to recognize Russian rule in Crimea and even started giving speeches in Belarusian.[10] A year later, in 2015, when Russia wouldn't submit to Lukashenko's request to lower gas prices, the Belarussian president began exploring closer relations with the West. Both Russia and Belarus had been hit hard by the downturn in fuel prices after doing business on a so-called oil-for-kisses arrangement: Moscow provided subsidized oil and gas; Minsk stuck to the Russian political line. Lukashenko's loan talks with the International Monetary Fund in 2016 were viewed by Moscow as a betrayal of this longstanding compact.

As the IMF talks indicated, Lukashenko was embracing new options. Around the same time, the EU lifted sanctions on Belarus, and Washington softened somewhat on its attitude toward Lukashenko's authoritarian rule. In retaliation, Russia has taken a hard line on Belarusian imports, banning meat, dairy, and various agricultural products; these are economic measures with real teeth, being that 40 percent of Minsk's exports go to Russia. Moscow has also cut oil shipments to Belarus. When Minsk announced visa-free travel for tourists from dozens of countries, Moscow retaliated by fortifying the border with Russian security forces.

In the past, the two nations have worked out their differences when there was any type of disagreement; they have always been close, if often contentious, partners. This time might be different, suggested Andrei Porotnikov, an analyst who writes for the Belarus Security Blog. "What the Lukashenko administration doesn't accept yet is that the Kremlin is only giving ultimatums now," he said. "Things aren't going to be resolved in the same way they previously were."[11]

Perhaps most ominously, Russian media have been escalating an information and propaganda war against Belarus. The Belarusian historian Nina Stuzhinskaya believes that the campaign is designed to whip up Russian sentiment against Belarus by fueling fears that the nation will become the next Ukraine—by betraying Russia and instead courting the West. When Stuzhinskaya went on a news program on Russian TV, she was struck by the contempt toward Belarus of the hosts and other guests. When she returned to Minsk, she said, a friend told her that she was glad that Belarus wouldn't go the way of Ukraine.

"I told her, 'you know what? In Russia's eyes, we are exactly like Crimea,'" said Stuzhinskaya. "And that's what's so worrying."[12]

* * *

As this book was going to press, Russia was planning to conduct a major military exercise with Belarus, called Zapad 2017, which observers believe will be the largest such exercise in post-Soviet history, with estimates suggesting that it might involve as many as a hundred thousand troops. Others worry that the Russians could use Zapad 2017 as a "Trojan horse" for potential annexation of Belarus.[13] That remains to be seen, but the exercise is, at minimum, a message to NATO and the Baltics that Russia's presence cannot be underestimated. That much-darker speculations—about annexation, for instance—have now become commonplace speaks volumes about the climate of intimidation and instability that Russia is creating.

CHAPTER FOUR

Diplomacy and Pressure
Russia's Backroom Dealings

After the Russian annexation of Crimea in March 2014, the EU, the United States, and Canada imposed economic sanctions on Russia that included travel bans and the freezing of assets. The sanctions, which extended to a second and third round of measures, have seriously weakened the Russian economy, especially in tandem with the drop in oil prices in 2014. In response, Putin imposed his own "countersanctions" on EU countries and the United States.

While the sanctions undoubtedly have hurt Russia, they have failed to stop Putin's aggression in Ukraine or to meaningfully alter his belligerent stance. Putin's determination to persevere and his insistence on Russian rectitude in Ukraine have rallied Russian pride and patriotism, while his hard-nosed economic diplomacy has exploited EU member nations' vulnerabilities and needs, helping to weaken their support for the sanctions regime.

In this effort, the Russians have made their biggest play for Mediterranean EU members, pushing trade ties and energy supplies. Putin used an official state visit to Greece to offer investment inducements—in return for the support of Athens for lifting the EU sanctions against Moscow. In Hungary, where support for Moscow is already strong, the Russians have tried to convince the government to support easing sanctions in exchange for Russian assistance in

speeding up nuclear-energy projects. In Italy, Russian countersanctions have taken a real bite out of the export economy—and as a
result, the Italian government has pushed the EU for an easing of
the sanctions.

Russia has also offered aid and comfort to anti-EU parties—
including a 9 billion euro loan from a Russian bank to France's anti-
EU party, the National Front. These parties sympathize with Putin
and Moscow and generally support the easing or lifting of sanctions.
The Russians have also expertly used online trolling and propaganda
to further weaken citizen support for the sanctions in EU countries.

Meanwhile, at the UN, Moscow is playing a shrewd and effective game of undermining American and Western efforts to resolve
wars and conflicts in Syria, Ukraine, and other nations. Putin's
men at the UN adeptly play on the Western democracies' hopes for
peace plans, by making symbolic but essentially meaningless con-
cessions and then using threats to gain their real objectives. A good
example came in September 2016 when Russian foreign minister
Sergei Lavrov and American secretary of state John Kerry seemed
to have hammered out an agreement halting hostilities in Syria.
Kerry anticipated taking the agreement to the Security Council for
ratification, a move that the Russians had suggested they supported.
But before it could get there, Russia helped destroy a UN aid convoy
by launching a missile attack that wound up killing twenty civilians
and destroying eighteen UN trucks carrying humanitarian aid. UN
secretary general Ban Ki-moon called the attack "sickening, savage
and apparently deliberate," and Washington made clear that it held
Russia responsible.[1] So much for the ceasefire.

The Russians have long had a policy of covering up human-
rights abuses committed by the Assad regime in Syria. Near the end
of 2016, at a Security Council meeting, after Ban discussed human-
rights abuses that the Assad forces were committing in Aleppo, the
Russian representative claimed that Moscow's own investigations
had found "not a single report of ill treatment or violations of international humanitarian law against civilians of eastern Aleppo." Then,

to add insult to injury, he accused Ban of getting his information from "fake news."[2]

Russia has used its UN veto power skillfully and ruthlessly, blocking eight UN Security Council draft resolutions on Syria since the beginning of the conflict. The resolutions have involved imposing a ceasefire in Aleppo; providing humanitarian aid; holding the regime accountable for human-rights violations; and imposing sanctions and starting investigations into Syria's use of chemical weapons against civilians.

Russia just as staunchly blocked UN action on Ukraine. The United States has warned that Moscow's "blanket use" of the Security Council veto could "jeopardize the security council's long-term legitimacy and could lead the US and like-minded countries to bypass it as a decision-making body."[3]

It's clear that Russia is more than happy to move Syria talks forward without American or EU input, and it has already taken steps to do just that. In March 2017, Foreign Minister Lavrov held talks in Kazakhstan on the Syrian conflict. His partners? Representatives from Turkey and Iran. The talks, which not surprisingly ended without any progress, illustrate how Russia is creating its own diplomatic channels.

Finally, Putin has strategically used the brouhaha around fugitive leaker Edward Snowden to keep Washington off balance and drive wedges among the Western allies.

Snowden is the National Security Agency contractor who, in 2013, stole top-secret documents and files and leaked them to the media; the files contained highly sensitive information on US domestic surveillance activities. Snowden was charged with violating the US Espionage Act and fled the country before he could face prosecution; he wound up in Russia, where he has been welcomed, and where he has recently been permitted extended residency until at least 2020.

Snowden remains a hugely divisive figure in the United States. Conservatives tend to see him as a traitor—for good reason, in my view. The materials he released may well have caused serious damage to America's national security interests. As Representative Devin Nunes, chairman of the House Intelligence Committee, said,

> Effective programs targeting foreign terror suspects were inaccurately portrayed as pervasive wiretapping operations to spy on American citizens and listen to their phone calls.... Among some people, this perception led to an increased suspicion of the intelligence community, which is unfortunate, since our intelligence professionals are doing really hard, important and sometimes dangerous work to prevent terror attacks.[4]

Liberals, on the other hand, see Snowden as a hero of civil liberties who has paid a serious price for exposing the national-security state. Remarkably, before Obama left office, more than one million people signed a petition calling on the president to pardon Snowden.

Putin knows this, and thus he has wielded his Snowden card, so to speak, with eagerness and skill. In February 2017, news reports suggested that our intelligence services had learned of Russia's potential interest in releasing Snowden into American custody. The idea, as the report had it, was that Putin would offer the American spy as a "gift" to win favor with President Trump. That would make quite a spectacle, especially since Trump, when he was still a private citizen in 2013, tweeted that "Snowden is a spy who should be executed."[5]

There may be nothing to the story, although most analysts think that Putin has gotten whatever he is going to get from the American defector at this point. Releasing him into American custody would make Putin look responsible and perhaps even interested in rebuilding the Russian-American relationship. But, as former deputy national security advisor Juan Zarate put it, it would also "no doubt stoke controversies and cases in the U.S. around the role of surveillance, the role of the U.S. intelligence community, and the future of privacy and civil liberties in an American context," and "all of that would perhaps be music to the ears of Putin."[6]

CHAPTER FIVE

Espionage
Spies, Leaks, and Cyberwarfare

Sometimes it seems that all the news in the United States regarding Russia involves spying, leaks, and cyberwarfare—and for good reason, as these topics have figured dramatically in recent American politics. From the 2016 campaign to the several investigations of the Trump administration's ties to Moscow, Russian cyberespionage and hacking has become one of the dominant foreign-policy issues of our time—and with good cause. Moscow's capabilities are formidable and seemingly expanding, and the confusion and disinformation that accompanies these attacks is a successful anti-American tactic in its own right. We may never know the true extent of Russia's role in the 2016 presidential campaign, but consider a different way of looking at it: Regardless of what Russia did or didn't do, Vladimir Putin made us believe that he was working behind the scenes to undermine our electoral process. The fact that we are launching investigations and questioning the integrity of our system is a huge win for the Russian leader. He sought to divide us, and he did. While we're divided and paralyzed, he advances.

This is not to say that it's all just perception. On the contrary, Putin's cyberwarfare makes its presence felt from the United States to Europe, from Norway to the Baltics—and he receives help in these efforts from Iran and North Korea, among others. A brief survey follows.

* * *

The most high-profile Russian-connected cyberattacks in recent years have focused on Ukraine and the United States. In Ukraine, Russian attacks have disabled the country's power grid and plunged it into darkness. In the United States, Russian cyberespionage, widely believed to be coordinated through Wikileaks, released thousands of private e-mails, many of them unflattering, from the Democratic National Committee, putting the party and its nominee, Hillary Clinton, on the defensive.

But these are only the best-known attacks. Moscow's cyberwarriors are busy elsewhere, too.

Take Norway. Oslo has been bracing for interference from its Arctic neighbor in Moscow since early 2017, when it welcomed three hundred US marines for service—the first time American troops had been stationed in the country since World War II. In retaliation for this and for Norway's adoption of EU economic sanctions against Russia in response to the Ukraine crisis, the Russians refused visas for two senior Norwegian parliamentarians.

In February 2017, Norway announced that a cyberattack had targeted the foreign ministry, the army, and other national institutions—including schools, the intelligence services, and a radiation-protection agency. The government suspected a Russian-linked group, APT29, or "Cozy Bear," the same one blamed for the American attacks. Cozy Bear is reportedly linked with the FSB, the Russian security service.

"Nine different email accounts were targeted in an attempt at what is called spear phishing," said Arne Christian Haugstoyl of Norway's intelligence service. Spear phishing aims to obtain passwords and other sensitive data by tricking users into installing malicious software on their computers.[1] The hack was "a serious attack on our democratic institutions," said Prime Minister Erna Solberg, although authorities did not think that the attack compromised classified information.[2] Given the deteriorating Russian-Norwegian relationship, further attacks would seem likely.

In the Baltics, meanwhile, Russian cyber-chicanery is a familiar topic, going back at least as far as 2007, when Russia took punitive action against Estonia. That year, the Estonian government in Tallinn decided to relocate a monument, the Bronze Soldier of Tallinn, dedicated to the memory of Soviet soldiers lost in World War II. Moscow wasn't pleased, and while it officially denied culpability in what followed, several officials would later take credit for it: a massive distributed-denial-of-service (DDOS) attack that crashed Estonian servers in banking, government, and the media. It's important to note that Estonia's information architecture was considered "some of the most advanced in the world at the time," according to *Geopolitical Monitor*.[3]

The Estonians have since become world leaders in defending against such attacks, but that hasn't stopped the Russians from striking elsewhere in the Baltics.

More recently, Russian hackers have launched a series of "exploratory" attacks against Baltic countries—focusing, ominously, on their energy networks. Estonia and its Baltic cousins Lithuania and Latvia are all linked onto the Russian energy grid, but all three countries have been looking to transition out of this arrangement into an energy partnership with the EU. You don't have to be a seer to guess how Putin looks upon such ideas. Security officials in Baltic countries believe that Russia is behind these attacks.

Moreover, Baltic security officials in the three nations say that Russian-backed hackers have launched additional "exploratory" cyberattacks over the last several years, focusing on energy networks. Some of the attacks are still being investigated, even though they took place near the end of 2015. They all targeted Baltic grids, like the malware attack that went after serial-to-ethernet converters (STEC), "which link sub-stations to central control," according to a Reuters report.[4] Around this same time, hackers launched a DDOS attack to disrupt operations on a Baltic electricity grid, although they failed to cause power outages. Another DDOS attack during this period hit a petrol-distribution system in an effort to disrupt fuel deliveries. This attack was also unsuccessful.

The saving grace of these attacks has been that they did not wind up causing any serious damage, but clearly that is their larger intention. "NATO and cyber security experts believe hackers are testing the Baltic energy networks for weaknesses, becoming familiar with how they are controlled in order to be able to shut them down at will," Reuters reported.[5] With the Ukraine example fresh in mind, the concerns run deep among Baltic leaders and security personnel.

"On a daily basis there are DDoS attacks designed to probe network architecture, so it could well be possible that something (serious) could take place later on," said a NATO official, speaking on the condition of anonymity to Reuters.[6]

One likely future target is Latvia, which finds itself in Moscow's crosshairs because it hosts a thousand NATO troops along the border that it shares with Russia. Many feel that the Latvian scenario will involve false-information campaigns, not only because that's the means most likely to sway the population against the NATO presence but also because Latvians might be susceptible to such appeals. More than one-quarter of the Latvian population is of Russian descent and nearly 40 percent speak Russian, making it a prime audience for Russian-language fake news and propaganda. Lithuania has already been targeted: the grid operator Litgrid says that attacks on the power grid and on other IT systems were "constant"—and it associates the majority of these attacks with Russian sources.

* * *

Putin's cyberwarriors have also busily intrigued in Europe, especially in the many critical elections that have taken place on the continent in 2017 and other political processes. In attacks from country to country, evidence points in the direction of Moscow's hacking expertise. Some observers think that Russian hackers may have played a role, or tried to play a role, in Britain's 2016 Brexit vote—an outcome favorable to Moscow.

The broad consensus among intelligence officials is that Russian hackers were quite active in the US presidential election later that year. And it seems that the warning that American intelligence officials sent in a postelection report—that Moscow "will apply lessons learned from its Putin-ordered campaign aimed at the US presidential election to future efforts worldwide"—has already come to pass in 2017.[7]

"German, French, British and Dutch security officials have all told me they've seen evidence of Russian efforts to influence their elections," cybersecurity expert James Lewis told the *Hill*. "It's not hypothetical."[8]

In February 2017, the *Moscow Times* reported that Russia had created "a new military unit to conduct 'information operations' against Russia's foes."[9] That sounds unambiguous, and Russian defense minister Sergei Shoigu helpfully offered more clarity when he said "propaganda should be smart, competent and effective."[10] There's no concrete evidence yet, but it appears that Russia attempted to destabilize the French elections in May 2017. As I was writing the manuscript in summer 2017, much speculation surrounded what role Russian hackers might play in the critical German elections of September 2017. Already, cyberwarfare had been making its presence felt as Chancellor Angela Merkel fought for her political future and for the vision of European unity with which she is so closely associated—a vision deeply at odds with the nationalist purposes of Vladimir Putin, with whom she has had a fraught relationship.

Trend Micro, a cybersecurity firm, released a report in April 2017 detailing how Russian hackers were setting their sights on the European elections. The firm found evidence of hacker intrusion into the servers of a German think tank closely associated with Merkel's Christian Democratic Union (CDU) party. The hackers' method was the familiar one of spear phishing.

In Holland, where in March 2017 Prime Minister Mark Rutte held off the challenge of nationalist Geert Wilders, security officials reported "hundreds" of attempts by hackers to break into the e-mail accounts of government officials.[11] In Bulgaria, officials believe that Moscow used fake news and other online ploys to swing the country's November 2016 election toward the victor and pro-Putin candidate, Rumen Radev.

Moscow's biggest focus seems to have been on the French elections, in which, by multiple accounts, the Russians took audacious steps of cybermischief. In the run-up to the general election on May 2, 2017, Moscow's cybersoldiers tried to break into the e-mail account of the frontrunner and eventual winner, Emmanuel Macron. Again, the method was spear phishing via e-mail. Macron's campaign manager believes that the hackers made "hundreds, if not thousands" of assaults on the campaign's databases and servers.[12] It's not surprising that they targeted Macron, who sees the EU as a bulwark against Russian machinations.[13]

The Russians also put to work other time-honored cybertools to influence French voting, including social media trolls and fake-news stories spread by Russian media sources like RT News and Sputnik. All of these tools were focused on discrediting Macron, with stories ranging from a gay relationship to ties with American financial firms, with Saudi Arabia, and with Hillary Clinton. Le Pen, meanwhile, who had promised to pull France out of the European Union if she won, seems to have been left alone.

Still, Macron won easily, in good part because these attacks did not appear to take hold with French voters. Some believe that one reason they did not is because the French president's campaign was much better prepared to deal with such sabotage than Hillary Clinton's was. Even so, the evidence of how hard the Russians tried to discredit Macron in an effort to defeat him should give all democracies pause. Elections are the crown jewel of democratic life, a kind of holy of holies: the Russians are trying to destroy electoral legitimacy in the Western democracies, an effort that serves the broader goal of fostering division within Western countries and splitting apart the Western Alliance.

* * *

Finally, there was the intriguing news in January 2017 that Russia had arrested two cyberspecialist intelligence officers and one computer-security expert and put them on trial for treason. Their crime? Sharing information with the United States. Official Russian news reports suggested that the men were being punished in the aftermath of the disclosure of Russian hacking activity of the US presidential election in 2016. Exactly what was happening here is difficult to untangle, but an important *New York Times* story by David Sanger and colleagues offered two compelling possibilities for the real reasons Russia took these steps: the first one speculating that Moscow could be "signaling that it might, however indirectly through a treason trial, reveal details of election hacking, which would have the potential to damage Mr. Trump's administration"; the second reason offering that "documenting a Russian role in the electoral hacks could also serve Moscow's foreign policy interests by underscoring the extent and power of the Kremlin's reach in the world."[14]

I'd bet on the second scenario, myself. In any case, the United States and its democratic allies ought to be prepared for much more of the same from Russia in the years to come.

PART TWO

FIGHTING BACK

CHAPTER SIX

Countering Russian Aggression

As this book goes to press, the world is still trying to understand the posture and policies the Trump administration will take on Russia. The signs are not encouraging: All indications have shown that candidate and now-president Trump does not prioritize Russia as a threat; nor has he planned any actions to counter the Kremlin. His infamous dismissal of Putin's likely elimination of his political opponents, saying that the United States killed people, too, shows a leader who seems unconcerned about Moscow. Moreover, the consistent message that Trump has sent our NATO allies is "pay your fair share" or else you might not be able to count on the United States.

There is room for some optimism, however. Trump's defense secretary, James Mattis, has no illusions about Russia or about Vladimir Putin. Moreover, National Security Advisor H. R. McMaster has long suggested that Russia is the most significant national-security threat facing the United States. McMaster is a first-rate mind: He largely devised the counterinsurgency strategy in Iraq that culminated in the surge. He is an historian and a man of great strategic vision and clarity. That he sees the Russian threat so clearly offers hope for a change of course.

* * *

"I personally believe that we need to consider lethal defensive weapons for Ukraine," said US Army General and Supreme Allied Commander Europe of NATO Curtis Scaparrotti. "They're fighting a very lethal, tough enemy, it's a Russian proxy, really...and the Russians provide some of their newest equipment there in order to test it."[1] He pointed out that Russian-led separatist forces continue to violate the ceasefire and that they are ratcheting up the incidents.

In September 2016, the House of Representatives passed the Stability and Democracy for Ukraine Act, which not only prohibits the US recognition of Russia's annexation of Crimea but also advocates a "comprehensive effort, in coordination with allies and partners of the United States" that would include "sanctions, diplomacy, and assistance" for the people of Ukraine. This would involve "lethal defensive weapons systems...intended to enhance their ability to consolidate a rule of law-based democracy with a free market economy and to exercise their right under international law to self-defense."[2]

That might sound provocative, but note that the act describes defensive weapons, not the offensive ones that would allow Ukraine to launch strikes against Russian or Russian-backed forces. The supply of defensive weaponry would almost certainly work to discourage separatist forces from further attacks and violations of the Minsk Agreement. These are important and achievable goals.

Ukraine needs to develop its own strategy to divorce itself from the "Russian world" and minimize the existential threat posed by Russia's invasion of Crimea and Eastern Donbas. It should aim to develop armed forces strong enough to deter Russian nonnuclear attacks, bolster its economy to support this military effort, and work toward independence from Russia on energy and security needs.

Finally, I agree with Alexander Vershbow of the Atlantic Council that President Trump should appoint a senior diplomat whose sole focus would be on negotiating directly with the Kremlin on the situation in Ukraine. All negotiations with the Kremlin should be predicated upon full and unequivocal implementation of the Minsk agreements and the restoration of Ukraine's sovereignty over its eastern territories. Should Putin not approve of a special appointment to aid in communication, the United States and its allies should, Vershbow wrote, "tighten sanctions and [step] up economic and military assistance to Ukraine...to protect their forces and deter new Russian offensives."[3]

* * *

At this late date, it is admittedly difficult to identify a constructive way forward in Syria, let alone to feel optimism about the prospects of any such plan. As we go to press, Russia, Turkey, and Iran are the power brokers in Syria, having instituted a shaky ceasefire, and each has significant leverage in some regions. The United States has gained a stronger hand—it potentially could, anyway—as ISIS has been forced out of territories that it once held. Colin H. Kahl, Ilan Goldenberg, and Nicholas A. Heras of the Center for a New American Security (CNAS) believe that the latest ceasefire, dating to summer 2017, represents an opening for the Trump administration to attempt to broker a broader and more permanent truce, and that Washington should be willing to work with Moscow to make this happen. They argue that once a stable national ceasefire is established, the United States and the other Syria players could work toward a political settlement—one in which, alas, Assad remains in office but power is slowly devolved away from Damascus.[4] I agree with this in principle, but, in my view, more skepticism of Russia is warranted here. The United States would need to satisfy its concern that Russia is legitimately interested in pursuing these goals and that verification can be established.

Elsewhere, the CNAS scholars go on to suggest that Washington should work with Moscow and Tehran to eradicate the remnants of ISIS and al Qaeda safe havens, although they acknowledge that trusting the Russians in this regard, especially after Syria's chemical attack in Idlib, will take some doing. I agree with them that the United States should stress that it will strike Assad again if there is another repeat of Idlib. I cannot say that I agree with their suggestion that the Trump administration should share targeting information with Russia as long as Moscow agrees to give "credible commitments to align air operations with the laws of war and to give Washington veto rights over targets," with the further suggestion that "U.S. support should be quickly withdrawn if Russia continues to bomb civilians."[5]

Finally, in one regard, I wholeheartedly concur with the CNAS scholars: they argued that "Trump should finally exercise the US's military and financial leverage to shape the outcome of the Syrian conflict and work alongside the EU, the UN and the wealthy Gulf States in the future rebuilding of Syria." This is absolutely correct. Syria is the starkest example of the failure of President Obama's "lead from behind" strategy. The United States sat out this great struggle, and many more have suffered in Syria who may not have had America stayed engaged. More than anything, this is my counsel in Syria: Engage. To date, I'm not persuaded that Trump has the interest or commitment to do so.

* * *

If President Trump and his defense team are serious about countering Russia, they must make dramatic, far-reaching, and sustained efforts to counter the country's hybrid-war brazenness.

Operationally, the United States and Europe need to make a concerted effort to regain the upper hand with Russia in the information war. The Russians have wrought havoc with their signal jamming and other systems hacks; much work needs to be done to better protect American communication systems. In turn, we need to turn our own considerable cyberwarfare capabilities more effectively against Moscow. Our offensive capabilities in jamming Russian communications systems must be made more robust.

Russia's formidable propaganda organs must also be countered. The United States should be much more aggressive—and confident—in refuting the reporting and assumptions of organs like

Russia Today, which exerts enormous influence. RT can and should be discredited. "The goal of an American-European partnership should be to create an alternative narrative to Russian propaganda, and disproving organizations like RT," wrote Caleb Larson, an analyst at Atlantic Expedition. "By combating these disinformation campaigns, the United States and Europe can create counter narratives to combat Russian propaganda and give an alternative perspective. Hopefully this would serve to reduce domestic Russian support of military adventurism in the Baltic countries and elsewhere."[6] Richard Weitz argued that the United States should amply fund its international broadcasting company Voice of America, and he called for a reconsideration of the shortsighted decision in 1999 to abandon the United States Information Agency.[7]

Weitz also recommended a comprehensive rethinking on the part of the United States and its European allies about how to fight the hybrid-war threat. He suggested that the United States and NATO develop unified security budgets. He also proposed that NATO must increase its capabilities for rapid deployment of security forces to vulnerable countries, and give each nation's armed forces critical reinforcement against the Russian threat.[8]

The Lexington Institute's Dan Goure called for aggressive modernizing of the US nuclear arsenal. He also argued that the United States should create a "cyber and electronic warfare capability to turn off the Russian power grid and information networks and acquir[e] the means to turn the Russian integrated air defense system into Swiss cheese."[9]

Will the Trump administration do any of this? If Trump himself has the will to pursue such objectives, he has the team in place to achieve them. McMaster, in particular, is certain to be much more hawkish on Russia than his predecessors. In 2015, after the Russian success in Ukraine, the US military devised a secret program, which McMaster headed, to figure out how the military should respond to the Russian threat. The program, the Russia New Generation Warfare Study, is meant to transform the US military's response in the face of threats through 2025. It "is intended to ignite a wholesale rethinking—and possibly even a redesign—of the Army in the event it has to confront the Russians in Eastern Europe."[10] Wesley Clark has described McMaster's efforts as the most dramatic shift in focus for the US military since the end of the Cold War.

"It is clear that while our Army was engaged in Afghanistan and Iraq, Russia studied U.S. capabilities and vulnerabilities and embarked on an ambitious and largely successful modernization effort," McMaster told the Senate Armed Services Committee. "In Ukraine, for example, the combination of unmanned aerial systems and offensive cyber and advanced electronic warfare capabilities depict a high degree of technological sophistication."[11] McMaster has made several trips to the front lines of Ukraine to see for himself how "hybrid warfare" has manifested itself.

* * *

Some argue that Washington should retaliate against Moscow for its INF Treaty violations by announcing new missile deployments or expanding missile defenses in Europe; others see that as counterproductive because of its potential to divide the European partners. At a minimum, the United States should use its bully pulpit to call out Russia on its violations and puncture Moscow's attempts to present itself as a constructive partner in nonproliferation. We should stop tiptoeing around the Russians and let them have it in a public forum. Another measure, suggested by Jon Wolfsthal of the Carnegie Endowment for Peace, would be to deny Russia the "right to fully exercise its rights under the Open Skies Agreement until such time as they return to compliance with the INF Treaty."[12] The Open Skies Agreement is an agreement among thirty-four nations to conduct unarmed aerial surveillance of one another in an effort to enhance transparency. Curtailing Russia's Open Skies freedoms would make clear that noncompliance carries penalties. These are just starter measures, however. A more comprehensive response to Russia's serial violations of the INF Treaty remains unformed.

The Russian buzzing of American planes and ships along with other provocations—like sending their subs to the borderline of international waters—are an effective tactic for Russia because they cost nothing to do and force the United States into a seemingly impossible choice: Would we seriously risk war in order to take action to stop such behavior? Some think that Putin does these things to distract attention from troubles at home; others see it as a message to Europe that the United States cannot be relied upon to protect its countries. Whatever the case may be, doing nothing carries its own risks: it emboldens Russia and reinforces its conviction that we want to avoid conflict more than anything else.

I agree with Howard Stoffer, a former State Department official, who recommended that the United States take a firm but proportional response to any further Russian provocations—like, say, "jamming the aircraft's radar and avionics systems—which could cause the aircraft to crash," as a CNN story summarized.[13] Would Putin go to war over such a thing? Unlikely, said General Michael Hayden. "Let me double down on another concept. The Russians really don't want to go to war with us. They are by far the weaker power."[14] The weaker power, that is, if and when the United States chooses to remind the Russians of this fact. Much hangs in the balance of whether the United States takes the necessary actions to do so.

* * *

Donald Trump has a chance to push back on Putin and turn the tide against Russia's ongoing campaign of aggression and sabotage. Trump's men are in place to do so, and good men they are. But in this area and others, the question remains: What does the president himself want to do?

CHAPTER SEVEN

A New World Oil Order

Even as Putin has used Russia's energy might in recent years as a tool of blackmail, the United States has its own powerful energy hand to play against such outrages—if it so chooses. If American political leaders should bring to bear the full power of the nation's energy potential, Russia will find, at a minimum, that its energy leverage is diminished. As such, it might yet find itself on the defensive.

The silver bullet in the American arsenal is shale natural gas and the new technology to extract it: hydraulic fracturing, or fracking. The United States, which once produced half the natural gas of Saudi Arabia and Russia, now has the capacity to equal those two nations' output—thanks to fracking. Before fracking, America had been an also-ran energy player. Now it has a seat at the energy table; it can be a global player in the energy markets. Our leaders should resist the efforts to curtail the production of this vital energy source, which has proved equally as environmentally friendly, if not more beneficial, as other forms of fossil-fuel production.

The magic of shale gas comes in its abundance and the relatively cheap cost of extracting it, especially with the improvements in fracking technologies. As the *Financial Times* put it: "Just compare an offshore well at $170m with a vertical shale well that costs under $5m, with a five-year payout for a successful deepwater well versus a mere five-month payout for a shale play. And multiply a single, individual shale well by hundreds of wells and hundreds of decisions and you get a new world order."[1]

It has happened quickly. Barely a decade ago, in 2005, the Energy Information Agency predicted that the United States would still be importing 25 percent of its gas in 2015; the rocket-like rise of shale gas has put the US in position to be a net exporter of gas by 2017.[2] The United States is now the world's leading gas producer. The rise of America as a shale-gas power has transformed the world energy market, eroding the power of OPEC, with which the US and Russia now share world leadership; the two countries and the organization currently account for 40 percent of "combined liquids production" worldwide. Before the rise of US shale, gas power in the world was held largely by the members of what was known as the Gas Exporting Countries, or GECF, dominated by Russia, Qatar, and Iran. Russian energy minister Sergey Shmatko called it the "gas OPEC."[3]

Shale gas has also put the United States on a different footing in regard to the Middle East and Russia—and it gives Europe a vital new option, too. The continent, with depleted reserves, has become a major importer of gas, getting about two-thirds of its supply in that fashion; of that amount, Russian gas accounts for about a half. Why would they want to deal with Gazprom, Putin's price gouging, and other machinations if a better alternative exists? "If the United States opens up the global gas market to unprecedented levels of transparency and competition, which its shale-extracted LNG [liquefied natural gas] exports appear capable of doing," wrote Anthony Fensom in the *National Interest*, "Russian President Vladimir Putin's influence in the region will further diminish."[4] Indeed, the United States has all it needs—political leadership remains the wild card—to become the world's energy superpower. Given how much Putin relies on energy economically and diplomatically, that development will be entirely to Moscow's detriment. Its ability to use gas to push around Bulgaria, Romania, Poland, and especially Ukraine, will be seriously eroded.

Further, LNG as a resource is becoming a bigger factor in the world energy market, with more and more countries becoming either importers or exporters of the fuel. For importers, LNG represents an alternate fuel source, often transported via alternate pipelines not controlled by Moscow. One key example of such alternate routes is known as the "floating pipeline," a supertanker that taps offshore gas sources at such volumes that it resembles an actual pipeline; unlike a traditional pipeline, however, the floating pipeline can move to new targets, operating at a fraction of the cost of the older arrangements. These new technologies give another edge to LNG in the energy market.

The United States has become an important player in the LNG market. In 2016, we began exporting LNG to Brazil, India, the United Arab Emirates, Argentina, Portugal, Kuwait, Chile, Spain, China, Jordan, and the United Kingdom. The inroads that the United States is making into these countries' gas markets represents a direct threat to the Russian presence—and not a moment too soon. Some European countries are still entirely dependent on Moscow for supplies. But in other countries, the impact of LNG is already changing the dynamic with Russia. In 2014, Lithuania built its own import terminal for natural gas; before that, it had relied on Russia for 100 percent of its gas supply. What impact did the new terminal have? It allowed Lithuania to negotiate a 20 percent discount on its next contract with Gazprom. In the past, such feats would have been unthinkable: If you pushed back on Gazprom, Gazprom would turn off the spigot (or threaten to). After the introduction of LNG, that threat wouldn't mean as much.

In April 2017, Gary Cohn, director of the White House's National Economic Council, said that the Trump administration would move faster on approvals for LNG export terminals—a hopeful sign for the future.

In short, on the gas front, technology and market demand are conspiring against Putin. The marketplace is fundamentally changing, and Russia's gas monopoly in Europe is not likely to survive in its present form. Moscow will always be a power player, but any lessening of its former stranglehold on what basically were, for many years, captive markets will change the economic realities. Gazprom won't be able to play such hardball on contracts, dictating the terms of long-term deals that give recipient countries no negotiability on price or other matters. It will have to make compromises, and those compromises will weaken Russia's ability to "weaponize" gas supplies in pursuit of its foreign policy goals.

Finally, the sanctions against Russia, though Putin has had success in working around them, are also causing some significant pain. I argued earlier that the sanctions alone won't cause Putin to alter his policies, but that doesn't mean that they don't hurt; Moscow unquestionably would like to see them lifted. Along with the drop in crude prices and the changes in the gas market, the sanctions have contributed to a challenging economic climate for Russia. In 2016, the number of Russians living in poverty reached almost twenty million people, more than 13 percent of the population, according to Rosstat, the government's statistical agency.[5] The Russian economy contracted in 2015 by 3.7 percent and by 0.8 percent in 2016.

Certainly, this contraction stemmed from several factors, including fluctuating fuel prices and the growing competition in the gas sector, but it's also likely that the sanctions have played a role. It's difficult to quantify their effect, but in 2015 the IMF estimated that US and European sanctions against Russia for its actions against Ukraine may have reduced Russian short-term economic output by as much as 1.5 percent.

Even Putin himself admitted, in 2016, that the sanctions have affected Russia. "Sanctions are hurting us," he said at an investment forum. "We hear that they are not a problem really, but they are, particularly with technology transfers in oil and gas. We are coping."[6]

Putin is the global expert at coping. He has taken a nation with a struggling economy, stagnant population growth, and an energy advantage whose best days are probably past and used his strategic political vision and sheer force of will to give Russia a global influence out of proportion with those liabilities. Whether wrestling with the sanctions or the growing competitiveness of the energy sector, Putin will surely adapt, exploit opportunities, and play his special brand of geopolitical poker. But when it comes to the energy sector, and particularly to natural gas, the Western democracies—especially the United States—are well positioned to thwart him.

CHAPTER EIGHT

Containment for the Twenty-First Century

C ontrary to President Trump's sometimes belligerent and often vacillating rhetoric, the strategy for containing and controlling Russian aggression begins and ends with reaffirming and fortifying NATO—rhetorically, politically, and militarily. President Trump should make unambiguously clear the United States' intention to perpetuate and bolster the alliance, and that America's longstanding commitment to defending its NATO allies remains in force. I share the view of Kimberly Marten, professor of political science at Barnard College, that the United States should sustain troop deployments in Poland—where we have recently added four thousand forces—and make clear to Moscow that these deployments are legal and internationally legitimate. Likewise, as Marten noted, we should urge our allies to honor their troop commitments in the Baltics and remind Moscow that these placements have past international precedent.[1]

There is some good news in terms of NATO commitments and the buildup. In addition to the Polish troop presence, the United States, along with Great Britain, Canada, and Germany, has begun deploying multinational battalion task forces to countries bordering Russia. According to early 2017 estimates, a total of 7,000 troops are deployed throughout the region, over half of which are from the United States. That includes the 4,000 US troops stationed in Poland; 1,200 troops in Latvia (consisting of a Canadian-led battalion with troops from Albania, Italy, Poland, Spain, and Slovenia); 1,200 troops in Lithuania (a German-led battalion with troops from Belgium, Croatia, France, Luxembourg, the Netherlands, and Norway); 800 troops in Estonia (a UK-led battalion with troops from Denmark and France); and forces stationed in Romania and Bulgaria.[2]

President Trump frequently criticized America's NATO allies during the 2016 campaign for not picking up their share of defense spending, and the United States still carries the lion's share of it. In 2016, the United States spent $66.41 billion on NATO military expenditures, dwarfing by ten times what the next-largest contributor, Great Britain, put in: $6.03 billion.[3] Some allies are stepping up their contributions, however, particularly in trouble spots: Defense budgets have risen in the Baltic States, where the Russian threat looms. Estonia, Latvia, and Lithuania will spend an estimated $1.9 billion in 2018, each doubling their budgets of 2005.[4] Estonia and Poland now meet the designated NATO minimum of spending 2 percent of GDP on defense; Latvia and Lithuania will meet the target by 2024.[5] Twenty-two allied nations have raised their defense spending.

I believe that a clearly signaled commitment from Trump to NATO, in line with the material commitments just mentioned, will send the right message to Putin without being too provocative. But that is not all. We should avoid any sense that we wish to go mano a mano with Moscow in conventional forces—not because we couldn't, if we had to, but because we shouldn't need to. We have other options.

These include asymmetrical capabilities, which the United States and NATO should act jointly and creatively to develop and publicize as deterrence against Russia. Marten encourages use of "cross-domain deterrence," in which one domain (land, air, cyber, trade, finance, or other) is used to deter threats in another. For NATO, this could include cyberpartnerships among NATO allies and "NATO-country cyber embassies on foreign soil," a model laid out by Estonia that makes cyberwar and land seizures in the Baltics less profitable for Russia.[6]

Sanctions against Russia have proved to be a useful (and cheap) tool for the United States, as Russian imports, exports, and direct investments make up a small fraction of the trillions of dollars of US foreign trade. (The cost would be higher for other NATO members.) Richard Haass of the Council on Foreign Relations argued for flexibility in how we design such sanctions. The goal, he wrote, is to "incentivize Russia not to do things that would undermine stability and as a result economic ties," but the sanctions should be designed such that they can be eased somewhat if the Russians modify their behavior.[7]

In June 2017, Congress voted 98–2 for new, tougher sanctions on Russia, seeking to punish Putin not only for his ongoing aggression in Ukraine, Syria, and elsewhere but also for Russia's attack on the American election system. Existing sanctions have taken a toll on Russia. I wholeheartedly support tightening the screws—and I can only hope that President Trump will have the wisdom to sign the bill.

Naturally, the Russians don't look kindly on our efforts to strengthen NATO. The growing deployments in Eastern Europe have not gone unnoticed by Moscow, which criticized the buildup as a "truly aggressive" provocation. When I argue for a stronger NATO, I do so with keen awareness of the volatility in Moscow and the dangers of unpredictable responses—we want to stabilize the situation in Europe vis-à-vis Russia, not explode it. The quandary, as Marten aptly put it, is that "being too aggressive could provoke Russian fears and lead to a militarized crisis, but being too passive could tempt Russia to take military action in the belief that it would be unopposed."[8]

Although he was often known for his "no drama" public persona, President Obama often seemed taken aback by Putin, not only in surprise but also in disgust at his geopolitical moves. Obama and his second-term secretary of state, John Kerry, often made pretentious pronouncements about what they deemed the Russian national interest. This kind of rhetoric achieved nothing except to feed Putin's determination and to make Foggy Bottom diplomats feel good. Fortunately, Trump shows no such inclinations. A calm, firm, even businesslike approach with Moscow—when appropriate—makes good sense. We should let Putin know that our primary concern is with his foreign-policy adventurism, not with his autocratic rule at home; we dislike the latter intensely, but we have little leverage to do much about it. We must focus on what is most important, and that is the stability of the Western Alliance.

To this end, leaving the moralistic rhetoric aside, we should stress empirical, measurable standards to which we expect Moscow's adherence. The United States and NATO should publicly clarify all interpretations of the NATO-Russia Founding Act and the 1999 Adapted Conventional Armed Forces in Europe Treaty, so that Putin understands that any new conventional military deployments must follow the interpreted limits of those treaty requirements. US foreign policy guided by "consistent, transparent, rule-based criteria" can help to "show respect for international laws and NATO allies, as well as ward off any Russian accusations of hypocrisy."[9]

We can also let Moscow know that neither Ukraine nor Georgia is anywhere close to meeting the requirements for NATO membership. Haass and others argue for making this clear to Putin; others see it as an unwarranted concession. My sense is that doing so would be wise if it were contained as part of a broader strategy of toughness and clear commitment to our *existing* NATO allies. In short, part one of our message to Putin on Ukraine should be: We're not looking to get the Ukrainians into NATO. We have enough troublesome partners.

We should couple that with a clear declaration that we won't accept Putin's expansion into Ukraine and reiterate our commitment to helping the Ukrainians protect their sovereignty. Deterrence, as

Haass aptly put it, adds up in the end to "the perception that a government is willing and able to defend its interests."[10] And the United States and NATO have a clear interest in halting Putin's efforts at further destabilization in Ukraine.

* * *

In Central Asia, the United States doesn't have a great hand to play. The countries in this region, which had a Westward orientation after the Cold War and for a time after 9/11, have moved closer to the Russian/Chinese orbit and will likely stay there for the duration. The United States has to take a fundamentally conservative approach here—a small-*c* conservative one—that stresses, to be frank, not making things worse. I agree with foreign policy scholars Eugene Rumer, Richard Sokolsky, and Paul Stronski that the United States has to pivot in Central Asia from the democracy-promotion and human-rights focus of the George W. Bush years to looking for "wins" where we can get them. Most likely, these would take the form of improved economic and social circumstances. Such improvements could lead to eventual political openings. But patience must be our byword in Central Asia.[11]

The Middle East—with the signature Putin move, of course, being his bold action in favor of Bashar al-Assad—is the area where the Russian leader's influence has grown the most dramatically in recent years. Here, the United States badly needs a much-sharper containment policy and outreach to our allies. Russia's move into Syria was its first incursion, militarily, into the Middle East since the disastrous Six Day War in 1973. In my view, Putin's triumph in Syria is one of the most successful gambles by a world leader in recent times, especially given the fact that concerted, American-led opposition would almost certainly have stopped him. Putin saved Assad's rule, which stands as a tragedy for the world and for the Middle East; he protected Russia's military base and port in the region; and he fostered a chronic state of violence, instability, and unpredictability.

Russian influence in the Middle East extends beyond Syria. As I noted earlier, the Russian rapprochement with Turkey represents another stunning Putin success. With the American estrangement from Turkey, Putin saw his opening—even in a country with which Russia had been at dangerous loggerheads not long before. The 2016 Syrian ceasefire, brokered by Turkey and Russia without American involvement, was a stark moment in recent history, a sign of American and Western incompetence and Putin's strategic shrewdness.

Possibly even worse is the Russian outreach to longtime American ally Egypt. Here again, Washington dropped the ball, refusing to make political accommodations for General Abdel Fattah el-Sisi—despite his staunch opposition to Islamists—and paving the way for Putin's opening. Russia and Egypt have signed their first arms deal since the Cold War, and Putin and el-Sisi meet regularly.

Putin has even tried to muscle into the most exalted American relationship of all in the Middle East: that between the United States and Israel. He has met many times in recent years with Benjamin Netanyahu, on everything from the situation in Syria to the Israeli-Palestinian peace talks to economic ties. "For us, Israel is an important partner in the Middle East," said Alexey Drobinin, deputy chief of mission at the Russian Embassy in Tel Aviv. "Why? Because we believe Israel is a vibrant economy, strong state.... We want Israeli technologies to be used to boost the Russian economy, such as in agriculture and hi-tech. Russia has something to offer in energy."[12] The frosty relationship between Obama and Netanyahu gave Putin the opening he needed. Putin has even endorsed making Jerusalem the Israeli capital; the United States has not.

In all these areas, the task at hand is something of a mirror image of our challenge in Europe and with NATO: we must shore up relationships with the fundamental allies with which we should never have become estranged, get assistance to those in alignment with our interests, and let Putin know that we're serious and committed to our strategy.

Shoring up Europe against Russia begins and ends with NATO; shoring up the Middle East against Russia begins and ends with the American relationship with Israel.

The US-Israel relationship took some real blows during the Obama years, during which the two allies often disagreed. Obama's coolness toward Israel and contempt for Netanyahu played no small part in that—and it is a shameful chapter in the president's legacy. But another factor is that the primary threats to Israeli security became more varied and complex. These include the rising power of Iran, the emergence of ISIS, and the growing problem within Israel's borders of an unhappy Arab population. Obama and Netanyahu famously disagreed on the Iran nuclear deal; the Israeli prime minister called it "bad in every aspect."[13] The two allies also could not get on the same page regarding Syria. Trump, however, clearly has a strong personal relationship with Netanyahu, and that's all to the good. Whether the personal dynamic will translate into a reinforcement of common aims and goals remains to be seen.

Defense cooperation between United States and Israel should be expanded. In September 2016, despite major disagreements on other topics, Obama and Netanyahu agreed to a new Memorandum of Understanding providing Israel with $3.3 billion annually in military financing and $500 million annually for missile defense.[14] Trump and Netanyahu should jointly commit to this new agreement and demonstrate a long-term support plan for Israel's security—and let Israel's adversaries know that, despite shifts in policy and administration, Washington's commitment to Jerusalem is unbreakable.

That's the first imperative. It looks to me like Trump is on a good path in this regard. But the broader challenge is how to handle a newly assertive Russia in this volatile part of the world. Again and again in recent years, we have been caught flatfooted by Putin's moves—a consistent theme not only of this brief book but of my previous work on Russia. In *Foreign Policy*, Ilan Goldenberg and Julie Smith imagined some disturbingly plausible future Putin adventures:

Might Russia support a major move South by the Assad regime towards the Jordanian and Israeli borders, thus taking on moderate opposition forces that have created a useful buffer zone for two key American partners? Could it significantly increase sales of sophisticated weaponry to Iran? Or might it move to dictate outcomes in Syria and Libya with two traditional American partners—Turkey and Egypt respectively—and by doing so cut the United States out of the process? To be sure, Russia is not going to annex territory in the Middle East but it could make a sudden move or a series of moves that would significantly undermine U.S. interests and present the United States with a fait accompli as it has already done in Syria.[15]

The situation is as complex and volatile as ever, but if there is anything that Washington policy makers should have learned from the events of recent years, it is that Putin doesn't follow our script or our expectations. Our strategic thinking has been woeful for years now; our ability to anticipate virtually nonexistent. We cannot afford this kind of incompetence in the Middle East. So, first: Let's repair and restore the US-Israel alliance. Second: Let's prepare for and anticipate future challenges from Moscow. They will come.

* * *

In March 2017, Curtis Scaparrotti, US Army general and supreme allied commander Europe of NATO, testified before the House Armed Services Committee on the Russian challenge to Europe and the Western Alliance. He reminded the lawmakers that Russia respects only strength, and that weakness would be seized on by Moscow to pursue its goals more aggressively. General Scaparrotti also had another message, one that bears remembering.

"Russia does respect NATO," he said. "It's one of the reasons that they're trying to undermine NATO and fracture it....Our enduring strength remains NATO, the most successful alliance in history." He went on: "The transatlantic alliance gives us an unmatched advantage over our adversaries—a united, capable, war-fighting alliance resolved in its purpose and strengthened by shared values that have been forged in battle."[16]

Some encouraging signs suggest that Scaparrotti's words are being put into action. In July 2017, the United States and allied forces in Bulgaria, Hungary, and Romania—totaling twenty-five thousand in all—conducted Saber Guardian, a ten-day military exercise designed to prepare our Eastern European allies for the growing Russian threat. It was the largest military exercise in Europe this year.[17] Also, in July, the United States deployed Patriot antiaircraft missiles in Lithuania, the first time that the US has brought these advanced systems to a Baltic nation. This suggests the willingness of America and NATO to come to the Baltic nations' defense if needed—since Latvia, Estonia, and Lithuania possess only short-range missile capabilities.[18] The American turn inward has been profoundly destructive, both in terms of weakening our position in the world—especially in Europe and the Middle East—and in giving previously unavailable openings to our adversaries. Yet for all the damage, the fundamental advantages that we possess remain profound. Not least among these are our alliances, which we have thoughtlessly allowed to atrophy during these dangerous years. Lest the years to come prove more dangerous still, it's time to strengthen these alliances. If recent military moves and exercises ordered by the Trump administration indicate a new American seriousness about—and engagement with—these threats, it's a change of approach that comes not a moment too soon.

CHAPTER NINE

Closer Allies, Clearer Goals

Russia has made considerable headway undermining the integrity of the international organizations and alliances that have historically formed the bedrock of the postwar order. General Sir Richard Shirreff, the former deputy supreme allied commander of NATO, observed that "the collapse of institutions built to insure our security" puts the European continent at serious risk.[1] Pushing back successfully will require a broad consensus not only in Washington but also among the Western allies. The key going forward is not American power and leadership alone but close American cooperation with our democratic partners, in Europe and elsewhere. We need these partners, and President Trump must do much better as a diplomat and a bridge builder than he has done until now. On his first European trip in May 2017, he managed to alienate many of our allies—whether by withdrawing from the climate accords or by refusing to make clear that he was as committed to NATO's principle of mutual defense as earlier presidents. He has so disparaged trade agreements, alliances, and other common staples of partnership among the Western democracies that some countries are making plans to go it alone, without America.

The clock is ticking on President Trump to change course with America's allies and shore up these vital relationships.

The key player in pushing back against Putin in Europe remains German chancellor Angela Merkel. She and Putin come from similar backgrounds. Both are from East Germany and are familiar with the German and Russian languages. Merkel's analytical mind and willingness to speak to Putin bluntly, along with Germany's preeminence on the continent, make Merkel the indispensable leader. She is also "the most steadfast custodian of the concept of the liberal West going back 70 years," said Strobe Talbott, who served as President Bill Clinton's head Russia adviser, "and that makes her Putin's No. 1 target."[2]

Merkel adamantly supports maintaining a powerful Europe to combat Russia—but she is unsure, to say the least, about Trump's commitment to that imperative. "The era in which we could rely fully on others is over to some extent," she said in May 2017, after the bruising trans-Atlantic summit. She suggested that it was time for Europe to "take our fate into our own hands."[3] Trump and Merkel will never get on as Merkel and Barack Obama did, but a powerful and unified American-German relationship is simply not optional in today's climate. I regard it chiefly as Trump's responsibility to make happen. If he is to be successful in Europe, he will need Merkel and Germany.

In his first meeting with Putin, France's new leader, Emmanuel Macron, demonstrated why the West will need him, too. A victim of both Russian hacking and propaganda during his campaign, he unequivocally established that two Russian news agencies—the state-controlled Russia Today and Sputnik—"were agents of influence which on several occasions spread fake news."[4] Most notably, he made this claim at a podium just a few feet away from where Putin was standing. Macron has condemned human-rights violations in Russia and has promised military repercussions for the use of chemical weapons in Syria. In France, too, Trump has a partner waiting on him to make the relationship work. But this relationship, too, has not begun warmly.

Britain has also been highly critical of Russia's involvement in Syria and the Russian backing of President Assad. Alongside the EU, Britain held the Assad regime culpable for the chemical-weapons attack in April 2017 and joined France and the United States in backing a UN resolution condemning the attacks and demanding that the Assad government cooperate with an international investigation into the event. Russia vetoed the resolution. The United States and United Kingdom should work together in Syria to negotiate a ceasefire and political agreement based on emerging zones of control.

* * *

Outside of Europe, other willing partners stand ready. Canadian prime minister Justin Trudeau and his foreign minister, Chrystia Freeland, have been vocal in their criticism of Moscow, especially regarding Syria and Ukraine. Trudeau's outspoken opposition to Assad's regime—he does not believe that any lasting peace agreement can include the dictator—clearly demonstrates Canada's ideological alignment with the United States in this area. Moreover, when US secretary of state Rex Tillerson journeyed to Moscow, Foreign Minister Freeland stressed that the secretary had "the full support of his allies and very much with the full support of Canada."[5]

In June 2017, addressing the Canadian parliament, Freeland said, "The fact that our friend and ally has come to question the very worth of its mantle of global leadership puts into sharper focus the need for the rest of us to set our own clear and sovereign course."[6] It was a clear reference to Trump and a clear sign of the growing exasperation with his posture toward even America's staunchest allies.

Australian prime minister Malcolm Turnbull, for his part, has declared that it is Russia's responsibility to keep Assad in line. "The Assad regime is a client state of Russia," he has stated bluntly, suggesting that Russia can and will be held accountable for what happens in Syria.[7] Even though Turnbull was notoriously on the receiving end of an unpleasant get-to-know-you phone call with Trump in January 2017, since then he has only demonstrated again why he is an essential partner to the United States. He played down tensions between the United States and Russia after the US cruise missile strikes on the Syrian airbase of Shayrat, saying that America had made it "very clear" that it was not "proposing to escalate or take further steps in the absence of any other action by the Syrian government."[8] If Trump cannot find a way to work constructively with Turnbull, it would be another bad omen for a strong prodemocratic Western alliance happening during his presidency.

* * *

The situation among our Asian allies is more complicated. Relations between Japan and Russia have been strained since World War II, though the two nations have made progress recently. South Korea and Russia have been at odds over Moscow's support for North Korea and Kim Jong-un.

Here, again, Putin shows his shrewdness, in that his deepening ties to North Korea, while broadly condemned, have recently played a key role in forcing Japan and South Korea to reach out to him. Japan's prime minister, Shinzo Abe, has looked to Putin for assistance in reducing the threat of a North Korean attack. The new South Korean president, Moon Jae-in, has also looked to Moscow to help ease tensions in the region—which have been plentiful, considering Kim's incessant nuclear saber rattling. Here is Putin's Machiavellianism at its most effective: Japan and South Korea find themselves drawn to Russia *because* of Moscow's ties to North Korea. Russia won't displace the United States as an ally for either of these nations. The thaw in relations between these two longtime American partners and Moscow, however, is another reminder of the centrality of North Korea's nuclear arsenal in global affairs—and how finding a resolution to it remains essential if we are to counter Putin.

* * *

It cannot be repeated enough: One of Vladimir Putin's central goals is to divide the Western Alliance. So far, he has had remarkable success. Yet, a concerted effort by the Western Alliance, working in unified fashion but with clear American leadership, would present a major threat to Putin's plans. This didn't happen during the Obama years because of the president's passivity, his "pivot" from Europe to Asia, and his conviction that "leading from behind"—which, in practice, meant not leading at all—was a new model for American foreign policy. It was an abysmal failure.

We haven't seen a unified Western Alliance so far under President Trump, either, but for different reasons. I am neither a Trump opponent nor a Trump supporter. I respect the president as the duly elected representative of the American people, and I wish him well, as I do for all presidents. I have written extensively that his election should not have been as surprising as it was for many people, and that some of his themes—such as a determined pursuit of America's national interest—are defensible and even commendable. But his stance so far toward the Western Alliance and NATO has been troubling, to say the least: His failure to endorse Article 5 of the NATO treaty left many of our oldest allies to question America's commitments, and his seeming dismissal of Russia's authoritarianism and antidemocratic behavior is disorienting to hear from an American president. I hope that as he settles into the job, he will come to understand definitively that Putin's Russia is not and cannot be an American ally—and that, in the struggle against him, America's democratic allies remain irreplaceable.

CHAPTER TEN

Empowering Cyber-Counterintelligence

F ew readers will require much convincing that the United States needs to improve its counterintelligence—especially in regard to the cyberhacking documented in so many major political stories of recent years. A decade ago, American counterintelligence primarily focused on how to stop terror plots, an imperative that remains unchanged. Sixteen years after the 9/11 attacks, however, any objective appraisal must conclude that the United States has done an excellent job in protecting the homeland against terrorism. The same cannot be said about intelligence theft, particularly in cyberspace.

We must do better.

Given the disasters of recent years, support has built for splitting off the US Cyber Command (known as CYBERCOM) from the National Security Agency, under which it currently operates in a "dual hat" structure under unified leadership; the director of both organizations is Admiral Mike Rogers. There are good arguments on both sides—but I believe strongly that we should sever the agencies at the earliest possible date.

Understanding the differences between the NSA and CYBERCOM is important for grasping the necessity of a split. The NSA's intelligence-gathering role is defensive: its mission is to "collect, analyze, and disseminate intelligence to national command authorities and decision-makers."[1] Legally, the NSA may only "steal" foreign intelligence; it may not attack, change, or disrupt someone else's network or information. Its work is covert, or at least it is supposed to be. CYBERCOM's mission, by comparison, is largely offensive. Its job is to "protect and defend U.S. computing assets and networks—in certain instances critical infrastructure—and to conduct the offensive missions when called upon."[2] Cyber Command operates to disrupt systems *overtly*—it doesn't mind if the enemy knows what it has done. In practice, the distinctions between the two branches can blur, because, in the dual-hat structure, the NSA has sometimes carried out offensive operations on behalf of CYBERCOM. Nevertheless, the defined missions are distinct.

CYBERCOM has operated only since 2009, but the centrality of its mission rapidly became evident. Before leaving office, President Obama signed 2017 National Defense Authorization Act, which provides for breaking CYBERCOM into a separate command and ending the dual-hat relationship. Splitting off CYBERCOM from the NSA would create an independent agency, solely dedicated to cyberoperations. Still, the break remains undone, and although it is likely, it is not a certainty. Even if it does happen, the timetable is unclear.

Many in Washington have expressed frustration at the slow pace at which the United States has developed effective tools, defensive but especially offensive, to work against the growth of sophisticated, audacious cyberattacks. "What seems clear," said Senator John McCain, "is that our adversaries have reached a common conclusion: that the reward for attacking America in cyberspace outweighs the risk. For years, cyber attacks on our nation have been met with indecision and inaction. Our nation has had no policy, and thus no strategy, for cyber deterrence."[3]

Advocates for the split see the missions of the NSA and CYBERCOM—intelligence-gathering, on the one hand, and combat functions, on the other—as being misaligned. Both would operate more efficiently if they were independent, with control over their own resources, the thinking goes. CYBERCOM operates subordinately to the broader spy operations of the NSA; its offensive approach could jeopardize the NSA's more subtle espionage operations. The two organizations operate under different legal authorities under the U.S. Code—a situation ripe for conflict. Having a dedicated, independent body devoted to cyberoperations is vital if the United States wants to counter Russian cyberaggression.

Yet McCain and others do not support splitting CYBERCOM off from the NSA, at least not yet. They think that the benefits of the dual-hat structure—especially in shared infrastructure and capabilities—outweigh the benefits of a breakup. McCain also sees the areas in which the two organizations overlap and worries that splitting them up would put them in conflict and reduce cooperation. Thus, many questions remain about resources, capabilities, and financing before CYBERCOM can be launched independently from the NSA.

Fundamental among these concerns is the creation and operation of a cyberplatform independent of the NSA, said the Strategic Command chief, General John Hyten. Hyten supports the elevation of CYBERCOM to an independent combatant command "sooner rather than later," but at the same time, he cautions that it should stay under the NSA rubric until the establishment of platform independence. "Once those capabilities are built, I would be supportive of separating the two," Hyten told the Senate Armed Services Committee. "But I will not advocate separating the two until we have a separate platform in the services that Cyber Command can operate on."[4]

These seem like sensible considerations, but they should not delay the splitting up of CYBERCOM and the NSA any longer than necessary, in my view. It makes sense for the break to come as soon as possible, considering the primacy of cyberthreats and the grave setbacks of recent years. Now that cyberwarfare has risen to an existential threat, America must have a fully resourced, completely autonomous Cyber Command. The Trump administration should establish one urgently.

* * *

Worries about the Russian cyberwar were heightened in December 2016 when Russia made a successful hack of the Ukraine power grid. The attack aroused concerns among American lawmakers that there would be a similar attack here and prompted calls for the incoming Trump administration to improve safeguards of America's critical infrastructure.

The Russians have already wrought havoc within American borders—witness the lingering political fallout from their cyberwarfare conducted during the 2016 presidential campaign. Before leaving office, President Obama shut down two Russian resorts in Maryland, calling them "beachside spy nests sometimes used by Russian intelligence operatives to have long conversations on the sand to avoid being ensnared by American electronic surveillance."[5] As was so often the case with Obama, it was a post facto move—the damage had already been done.

Looking forward, we must expect more Russian attacks. How to respond? The United States can retaliate on many levels.

A low-level cyberretaliation might send encrypted cyberweapons into Russian networks; it might involve, according to the *Yale Journal of International Affairs*, the "defacements of government websites, disruptions of Internet services, interferences and disablements of communications, or the dissemination of propaganda." The *Yale* article also discloses that after the Russian hacking of DNC databases, senior government officials considered embedding malware in Russian computer systems "for intelligence gathering and future cyber-assaults."[6]

A medium-level cyberintrusion might use "logic bombs"—computer code inserted into software systems to set off malfunctions—to cause operational damage to Russia's critical infrastructure. The United States has invested significantly in this option. A high-level cyberattack would simply up the ante, striking the most critical

Russian infrastructure in the most serious ways—say, by hacking and disabling air-traffic-control systems, an event that could lead to loss of life.[7] Finally, in a military-level cyberattack, the United States could launch direct attacks on Russian military targets, by, say, disabling power at airfields or nuclear facilities. Needless to say, higher-level responses would likely bring retaliation or attempted retaliation. Yet the United States has clearly pondered taking such steps: we implanted malware in Russian military systems during the 2016 election for potential activation (although it appears that we didn't go through with the attack).

The potentially stark ramifications of these options are clear. Yet the Russian incursions into our own systems have been quite serious as well—as are the threats of further attacks.

* * *

Finally, we've got to do better on counterintelligence more generally. At every turn over the last several years, we have been caught unawares and unprepared for Russian actions. The aggression against Crimea and Ukraine, the bold moves in Syria and the Middle East, and the cyberwar taken to American shores—all these Putin campaigns essentially went undetected by American intelligence.

To some degree, Putin's routs of recent years happened because of the lack of American attention. While Putin operated with boldness and determination, American intelligence still largely trained its eyes only on counterterrorism. We simply didn't focus on the Russian threat.

I've argued for years that we should be channeling more resources into US spy agencies, and fortunately, that finally seems to be happening: US intelligence agencies have heightened their operations against Russia to a pitch not seen since the close of the Cold War, according to officials. This mobilization includes "clandestine CIA operatives, National Security Agency cyberespionage capabilities, satellite systems and other intelligence assets," according to a report in the *Washington Post*.[8]

Still, US spy agencies are "playing catch-up big time" with

Russia, said a senior US intelligence official.[9] Another acknowledged that "we've definitely been ignoring Russia for the last 15 years."[10] We have a long way to go, though the arrow is finally pointing in the right direction.

One liability of the climate in which the United States operates—which does not burden Russia—consists of the opposing viewpoints of privacy advocates and defenders of strong counterintelligence. This is particularly evident in the debate over section 702 of the Foreign Intelligence Surveillance Act of 1978, which will expire in December 2017 unless Congress reauthorizes it—something it absolutely should do.

Section 702 permits the United States to, in the words of one description, "spy on foreigners believed to be living overseas whose communications pass through American phone or internet providers." It is a powerful tool, but privacy advocates complain that it inevitably gathers up vast amounts of data on innocent Americans. A bipartisan group of lawmakers in Washington is working on revisions to the law to address these concerns and ensure that the law will be reauthorized; some question, however, whether the Trump administration will get behind a new, possibly weakened, version of the law.[11]

We should heed the words of Mike Rogers, head of CYBERCOM, who believes that letting section 702 expire would seriously compromise cyberintelligence operations. Rogers avers that without section 702, we might not have learned what we have so far about Russian interference in the 2016 election. "Much of what was in the intelligence community's assessment, for example, on the Russian efforts against the U.S. election process in 2016, was informed by knowledge we gained through (Section) 702 authority," he said.[12]

That testimony may not be the most inspiring argument for preserving the law—that it helped us diagnose, after the fact, what Russia was up to—but this is no time for the United States to scale back its tool kit. Reauthorizing section 702 will only be a small aspect of what needs to be a broad and committed American cyber-counterintelligence strategy against Russia—a strategy that, invariably, will have to begin incorporating offensive moves as much as defensive ones.

Notes

Introduction

1 David French, "How Russia Wins," *National Review*, December 12, 2016, http://www.nationalreview.com/article/442980/vladimir-putins-russia-strategy-how-russia-wins.

2 Jonathon Morgan, quoted in Scott Shane, "Purged Facebook Page Tied to the Kremlin Spread Anti-Immigrant Bile," *New York Times*, September 12, 2017, https://www.nytimes.com/2017/09/12/us/politics/russia-facebook-election.html?action=click&contentCollection=Politics&module=Related Coverage&region=EndOfArticle&pgtype=article.

3 Barack Obama and Mitt Romney, quoted in Stephanie Condon and Jake Miller, "Fact-Checking the Final Presidential Debate," CBS News, October 23, 2012, https://www.cbsnews.com/news/fact-checking-the-final-presidential-debate/.

4 Quoted in Pete Baumgartner and Rikard Jozwiak, "Putin Arrives in Budapest amid Concerns over EU Unity," Radio Free Europe/Radio Liberty, February 2, 2017, https://www.rferl.org/a/putin-russia-hungary-orban-european-union-concerns-trump-sanctions/28273592.html.

5 Donald J. Trump, quoted in Ashley Parker, "Trump Says NATO Is 'Obsolete,' UN Is 'Political Game,'" *New York Times*, April 2, 2016, https://www.nytimes.com/politics/first-draft/2016/04/02/donald-trump-tells-crowd-hed-be-fine-if-nato-broke-up/.

6 Tom Ridge, quoted in Madeleine Sheehan Perkins, "Former Homeland Security Chief: 'Trump Talks about Winning—Right Now, Putin Is Winning,'" *Business Insider*, March 23, 2017, http://www.businessinsider.com/tom-ridge-trump-putin-russia-2017-3.

7 Charles Krauthammer, quoted in "Krauthammer's Take: Russians Disproved Obama's Mantra That 'You Can't Win a Civil War Militarily,'" *National Review*, December 30, 2016, http://www.nationalreview.com/corner/443442/russia-wins-syria-america-shut-out-obama-embarrassed-putin.

8 Judy Dempsey, "Does Russia Divide Europe?," Carnegie Europe, October 26, 2015, http://carnegieeurope.eu/2015/10/26/does-russia-divide-europe-pub-61780.

9 Rosen Plevneliev, quoted in Gordon Corera, "Bulgaria Warns of Russian

Attempts to Divide Europe," BBC, November 4, 2016, http://www.bbc.com/news/world-europe-37867591.

10 Rosen Plevneliev, quoted in ibid.

11 Shehab Khan, "Trump, Putin and Erdogan a 'Ring of Autocrats' Trying to Destroy Europe, Says EU's Chief Brexit Negotiator," *Independent*, November 22, 2016, http://www.independent.co.uk/news/world/europe/donald-trump-vladimir-putin-president-erdogan-russia-turkey-europe-threat-guy-verhofstad-a7432206.html.

12 Guy Verhofstadt, quoted in ibid.

13 Barack Obama, quoted in "Remarks by President Obama and Prime Minister Erdogan of Turkey after Bilateral Meeting" (meeting, Grand Hyatt Hotel, Seoul, March 25, 2012), White House: President Barack Obama, https://obamawhitehouse.archives.gov/the-press-office/2012/03/25/remarks-president-obama-and-prime-minister-erdogan-turkey-after-bilatera.

14 Vladimir Putin, quoted in Isabel Hunter, "Strangely Enough, It's US Relations with Turkey That Could Suffer Most after the Assassination of the Russian Ambassador," *Independent*, December 20, 2016, http://www.independent.co.uk/voices/turkey-ankara-russian-ambassador-assassination-us-relations-vladimir-putin-a7486251.html.

15 Vladimir Putin, quoted in Ting Shi and Ilya Arkhipov, "Bromance between Xi and Putin Grows as U.S. Spats Escalate," Bloomberg, October 13, 2016, https://www.bloomberg.com/news/articles/2016-10-13/xi-putin-bromance-grows-in-security-bond-as-u-s-spats-escalate.

16 Donald Trump, quoted in Peter Baker and Choe Sang-Hun, "Trump Threatens 'Fire and Fury' against North Korea If It Endangers U.S.," *New York Times*, August 8, 2017, https://www.nytimes.com/2017/08/08/world/asia/north-korea-un-sanctions-nuclear-missile-united-nations.html?_r=0.

17 William J. Broad and David E. Sanger, "North Korea's Missile Success Is Linked to Ukrainian Plant, Investigators Say," *New York Times*, August 14, 2017, https://www.nytimes.com/2017/08/14/world/asia/north-korea-missiles-ukraine-factory.html?hp&action=click&pgtype=Homepage&clickSource=story-heading&module=first-column-region&region=top-news&WT.nav=top-news&_r=2.

18 Kim Jong-un, quoted in Elizabeth Shim, "North Korea: Russia's Putin Sent Kim Jong Un Congratulatory Message," United Press International, August 15, 2017, http://www.upi.com/Top_News/World-News/2016/08/15/North-Korea-Russias-Putin-sent-Kim-Jong-Un-congratulatory-message/4891471272780/.

19 Vladimir Putin, quoted in John Bacon, "Putin Meets with Iranian Leader, Touts 'Reliable and Stable Partner,'" *USA Today*, March 28, 2017, https://www.usatoday.com/story/news/world/2017/03/28/putin-meets-iranian-leader-touts-reliable-and-stable-partner/99723886/.

20 "Gen. Keane: Russia Moving Arms through Iran to Taliban in

Afghanistan," Fox News, April 25, 2017, http://insider.foxnews.com/
2017/04/25/jack-keane-russia-arming-taliban-sending-weapons-through-
iran.

21 Vladimir Putin, quoted in Paul McCleary, "Putin and Trump Talk Up
Need for More Nuclear Weapons," *Foreign Policy*, December 22, 2016,
http://foreignpolicy.com/2016/12/22/putin-and-trump-talk-up-need-for-
more-nuclear-weapons/.

22 Vladimir Putin, quoted in Mark Hensch, "Putin: Russia Must Strengthen
Its Nuclear Arms," *Hill*, December 22, 2016, http://thehill.com/policy/
international/russia/311536-putin-russia-must-strengthen-its-nuclear-arms.

23 Dmitry Kiselev, quoted in "The Threat from Russia," *Economist*, October
22, 2016, https://www.economist.com/news/leaders/21709028-how-contain-
vladimir-putins-deadly-dysfunctional-empire-threat-russia.

24 *Washington Post*, quoted Latika Bourke, "Russia's Opposition Leader
Arrested as Anti-Putin Protests Sweep Russia," *Sydney Morning Herald*,
March 27, 2017, http://www.smh.com.au/federal-politics/political-opinion/
russias-opposition-leader-arrested-as-antiputin-protests-sweep-russia-
20170326-gv6xme.html.

25 Liz Wahl, quoted in Justin Baragona, "Ex-Russia Today Anchor: 'The
Goal of Russian Media Is to Undermine Faith in Our Institutions,'"
Mediaite, December 11, 2016, https://www.mediaite.com/online/ex-russia-
today-anchor-the-goal-of-russian-media-is-to-undermine-faith-in-our-
institutions/.

26 Gallup, quoted in John D. Davidson, "Russia Isn't Trying to Elect Trump,
It's Trying to Undermine America's Faith in Elections," *Federalist*,
September 6, 2016, http://thefederalist.com/2016/09/06/russia-is-trying-to-
undermine-americas-faith-in-elections/.

27 Abby Phillip, "O'Reilly Told Trump That Putin Is a Killer. Trump's Reply:
'You Think Our Country Is So Innocent?,'" *Washington Post*, February 4,
2017, https://www.washingtonpost.com/news/post-politics/wp/2017/02/04/
oreilly-told-trump-that-putin-is-a-killer-trumps-reply-you-think-our-
countrys-so-innocent/?utm_term=.8b68049da86b.

28 Secured Borders, quoted in Scott Shane, "Purged Facebook Page."

29 Jonathon Morgon, quoted in ibid.

30 Douglas E. Schoen and Evan Roth Smith, *Putin's Master Plan: To Destroy
Europe, Divide NATO, and Restore Russian Power and Global Influence* (New
York: Encounter Books, 2016), 138.

Chapter 1

1 Quoted in "Kiev and Kremlin Trade Blame over Surge in Fighting in
East Ukraine," *Guardian*, January 31, 2017, https://www.theguardian.com/
world/2017/jan/31/kiev-and-kremlin-trade-blame-surge-in-fighting-in-east-
ukraine-russia-backed-rebels.

2 Petro Poroshenko, quoted in "More Than Ten Killed and Dozens Injured in Surge of Violence in East Ukraine," *Telegraph*, January 31, 2017, http://www.telegraph.co.uk/news/2017/01/31/ten-killed-dozens-injured-surge-violence-east-ukraine/.

3 Peter Maurer, quoted in Nolan Peterson, "Nolan Peterson: The Trench War Being Waged on Europe's Doorstep," *Newsweek*, April 9, 2017, http://www.newsweek.com/nolan-peterson-trench-war-being-waged-europes-doorstep-580094.

4 Dina Gusovsky, "Proxy Warriors: 4 Types of Pro-Russian Separatists," CNBC, July 23, 2014, https://www.cnbc.com/2014/07/23/pro-russian-separatists-in-ukraine-putins-politics-get-complicated.html.

5 Henry Meyer, Ilya Arkhipov, Stepan Kravchenko, and Yuliya Fedorinova, "Putin Quietly Detaches Ukraine's Rebel Zones as U.S. Waffles," Bloomberg, April 19, 2017, https://www.bloomberg.com/news/articles/2017-04-20/putin-quietly-detaches-ukraine-s-rebel-zones-as-u-s-waffles.

6 *Maritime Doctrine of the Russian Federation 2020*, quoted in "The Link between Putin's Military Campaigns in Syria and Ukraine," *Atlantic*, October 2, 2015, https://www.theatlantic.com/international/archive/2015/10/navy-base-syria-crimea-putin/408694/.

7 "Putin Signs Syria Base Deal, Cementing Russia's Presence There for Half a Century," Reuters, July 27, 2017, https://www.reuters.com/article/us-mideast-crisis-russia-syria/putin-signs-syria-base-deal-cementing-russias-presence-there-for-half-a-century-idUSKBN1AC1R9.

8 "Russia/Syria: War Crimes in Month of Bombing Aleppo," Human Rights Watch, December 1, 2016, https://www.hrw.org/news/2016/12/01/russia/syria-war-crimes-month-bombing-aleppo.

9 Dmitry Medvedev, quoted in Tom Batchelor, "Russia Says US Air Strikes in Syria Came 'within an Inch' of Military Clash with Their Forces," *Independent*, April 7, 2017, http://www.independent.co.uk/news/world/middle-east/russia-us-air-strikes-syria-russia-within-inch-military-clash-war-dmitry-medvedev-prime-minister-a7672791.html.

10 Nikki R. Haley, quoted in Somini Sengupta, "Russia Vetoes U.N. Resolution Condemning Syria Chemical Attack," *New York Times*, April 12, 2017, https://www.nytimes.com/2017/04/12/world/middleeast/united-nations-resolution-syria-russia-united-states.html?mtrref=undefined.

11 Andrius Sytas, "Lithuania Says Russia Has Ability to Launch Baltic Attack in 24 Hours," Reuters, April 3, 2017, http://www.reuters.com/article/us-lithuania-russia-idUSKBN1750Z0.

12 Eric Schmitt, "U.S. Lending Support to Baltic States Fearing Russia," *New York Times*, January 1, 2017, https://www.nytimes.com/2017/01/01/us/politics/us-baltic-russia.html?mtrref=undefined.

13 Raymond T. Thomas, quoted in ibid.

14 Anna Nemtstova, "The Baltics Try to Wall Out Russian Agents, But Moscow's Message Still Comes Through," *Daily Beast*, July 11, 2017, http://www.thedailybeast.com/russias-fear-abroad-the-baltics-try-to-wall-out-russian-agents-but-moscows-message-still-comes-through.

15 United Russia, quoted in BIRN Team, "Putin's Party Signs 'Military Neutrality' Agreements with Balkan Parties," Medium, June 29, 2016, https://medium.com/@balkaninsight/putins-party-signs-military-neutrality-agreements-with-balkan-parties-8f2bbad4c23.

16 US Army, quoted in Richard Weitz, "Countering Russia's Hybrid Threats," *Diplomaatia*, November 2014, https://www.diplomaatia.ee/en/article/countering-russias-hybrid-threats/.

17 Valery Gerasimov, quoted in Fiona Hill, "Hybrid War: The Real Reason Fighting Stopped in Ukraine—For Now," Reuters, February 26, 2015, http://www.reuters.com/article/idIN55467880620150226.

18 Anders Fogh Rasmussen, quoted in Damien Sharkov, "Russia Engaging in 'Hybrid War' with Europe, Says Former NATO Chief," *Newsweek*, April 15, 2015, http://www.newsweek.com/2015/04/24/former-nato-chief-says-europe-hybrid-war-putin-322293.html.

19 *Georgian Journal*, quoted in Will Cathcart, "Putin Uses the S-300 Missile to Dominate Its Neighbors. Now Iran Can, Too," *Daily Beast*, April 15, 2015, http://www.thedailybeast.com/putin-uses-the-s-300-missile-to-dominate-its-neighbors-now-iran-can-too.

20 James Kirchick, "The Road to a Free Europe Goes through Moscow," *POLITICO*, March 17, 2017, http://www.politico.com/magazine/story/2017/03/russias-plot-against-the-west-214925.

21 Paul Selva, quoted in Michael R. Gordon, "Russia Has Deployed Missile Barred by Treaty, U.S. General Tells Congress," *New York Times*, March 8, 2017, https://www.nytimes.com/2017/03/08/us/politics/russia-inf-missile-treaty.html.

22 Vladimir Putin, quoted in Michael R. Gordon, "Russia Deploys Missile, Violating Treaty and Challenging Trump," *New York Times*, February 14, 2017, https://www.nytimes.com/2017/02/14/world/europe/russia-cruise-missile-arms-control-treaty.html?mcubz=0.

23 Philip M. Breedlove, quoted in Michael R. Gordon, "NATO Commander Says He Sees Potent Threat from Russia," *New York Times*, April 2, 2014, https://www.nytimes.com/2014/04/03/world/europe/nato-general-says-russian-force-poised-to-invade-ukraine.html?mcubz=0.

24 "Russian Spy Ship Returns off U.S. Coast, Near Sub Base," CBS News, March 15, 2017, https://www.cbsnews.com/news/russian-spy-ship-viktor-leonov-us-east-coast-georgia-navy-submarine-base/.

Chapter 2

1 Oilprice.com, "U.S. to Undermine Russia's Gas Monopoly in Europe," NASDAQ, April 25, 2016, http://www.nasdaq.com/article/us-to-undermine-russias-gas-monopoly-in-europe-cm610811.

2 Zainab Calcuttawala, "How Russia Is Using Oil Deals to Secure Its Influence in the Middle East," Oilprice.com, February 26, 2017, http://oilprice.com/Energy/Energy-General/How-Russia-Is-Using-Oil-Deals-To-Secure-Its-Influence-In-The-Middle-East.html.

3 Chris Weafer, quoted in Salma El Wardany, Stephen Bierman, and Bruce Stanley, "Rosneft Expands in Middle East with Libya and Iraq Oil Deals," Bloomberg, February 21, 2017, https://www.bloomberg.com/news/articles/2017-02-21/rosneft-signs-libya-oil-deal-as-more-investors-return-to-country.

4 "Nord Stream 2," Gazprom, n.d., http://www.gazprom.com/about/production/projects/pipelines/built/nord-stream2/.

5 James Marson, "Putin Exploits Europe's Divisions in Bid to Dominate Gas Supply," *Wall Street Journal*, March 30, 2017, https://www.wsj.com/articles/putin-exploits-europes-divisions-in-bid-to-dominate-gas-supply-1490866203.

6 Vladimir Putin, quoted in ibid.

7 Ibid.

8 Peter Hultqvist, quoted in ibid.

9 Emre Peker, "EU Says It Can't Block Russia-Backed Nord Stream 2 Pipeline," *Wall Street Journal*, March 30, 2017, https://www.wsj.com/articles/eu-says-it-cant-block-russia-backed-nord-stream-2-pipeline-1490906474.

10 "Southern Gas Corridor," Trans Adriatic Pipeline, n.d., https://www.tap-ag.com/the-pipeline/the-big-picture/southern-gas-corridor.

11 Alissa de Carbonnel and Oleg Vukmanovic, "EU Gets Wake-Up Call as Gazprom Eyes Rival Tap Pipeline," Reuters, February 14, 2017, http://www.reuters.com/article/us-gazprom-eu-tap-idUSKBN15T1LC.

12 Quoted in ibid.

Chapter 3

1 Camilla Hagelund, quoted in Damien Sharkov, "Putin Buddies Up to Central Asia Leaders on His Trip across the Region," *Newsweek*, March 2, 2017, http://www.newsweek.com/here-what-we-learned-putin-mini-tour-through-central-asia-562263.

2 Vladimir Putin, quoted in Catherine Putz, "Touring the Backyard: Putin Pays Central Asia a Visit," *Diplomat*, March 1, 2017, http://thediplomat.com/2017/03/touring-the-backyard-putin-pays-central-asia-a-visit/.

3 Lilit Gevorgyan, quoted in Sharkov, "Putin Buddies Up to Central Asia Leaders."

4 Darren Goode, "Pipeline to Bypass Russia Pushed," *POLITICO*, April 18, 2014, http://www.politico.com/story/2014/04/gas-pipeline-bypass-russia-105786#ixzz2zBH0tj3e.

5 Samuel Ramani, "The Implications of Tightening Russia-Uzbekistan Ties," *Diplomat*, May 11, 2016, http://thediplomat.com/2016/05/the-implications-of-tightening-russia-uzbekistan-ties/.

6 Shavkat Mirziyoyev, quoted in Catherine Putz, "Uzbek President Mirziyoyev Makes State Visit to Russia," *Diplomat*, April 7, 2017, http://thediplomat.com/2017/04/uzbek-president-mirziyoyev-makes-state-visit-to-russia/.

7 Igor Dodon, quoted in Andrew Rettman, "Moldova Turns from EU to Russia," *euobserver*, January 18, 2017, https://euobserver.com/foreign/136582.

8 Alexander Lukashenko, quoted in Lidia Kelly, "Belarus President Alexander Lukashenko: 'Better to Be a Dictator Than Gay,'" *HuffPost*, May 4, 2012, http://www.huffingtonpost.com/2012/03/04/belarus-lukashenko-dictator-gay-comments_n_1319829.html.

9 Schoen and Smith, *Putin's Master Plan*, 16.

10 Chris Miller, "Belarus and the Failure of the Russian World," *American Interest*, April 4, 2017, https://www.the-american-interest.com/2017/04/04/belarus-and-the-failure-of-the-russian-world/.

11 Andrei Porotnikov, quoted in Sabra Ayres, "In Belarus, a Rising Fear: Will We Be the Next Ukraine?," *Los Angeles Times*, March 8, 2017, http://www.latimes.com/world/la-fg-belarus-russia-relations-20170308-story.html.

12 Nina Stuzhinskaya, quoted in ibid.

13 Jeff Daniels, "Large-Scale Russian Military Exercises in Belarus Feared to Be Set-Up for Putin's Next Conquest," CNBC, August 19, 2017, https://www.cnbc.com/2017/08/19/fears-grow-russian-military-drills-in-belarus-are-moscows-next-crimea.html.

Chapter 4

1 Ban Ki-moon, quoted in Julian Borger and Spencer Ackerman, "Ban Ki-Moon Condemns 'Apparently Deliberate' Syria Aid Convoy Attack," *Guardian*, September 20, 2016, https://www.theguardian.com/world/2016/sep/20/un-suspends-all-aid-convoy-movements-in-syria-after-airstrike.

2 Quoted in Sarah Begley, "Read the Full Text of Samantha Power's Scathing Speech on Russia," *TIME*, January 17, 2017, http://time.com/4637117/samantha-power-united-nations-russia-speech-transcript/.

3 Julian Borger and Bastien Inzaurralde, "Russian Vetoes Are Putting UN Security Council's Legitimacy at Risk, Says US," *Guardian*, September 23, 2015, https://www.theguardian.com/world/2015/sep/23/russian-vetoes-putting-un-security-council-legitimacy-at-risk-says-us.

4 Devin Nunes, quoted in Julian Hattem, "Spying after Snowden: What's Changed and What Hasn't," *Hill*, December 25, 2016, http://thehill.com/

policy/technology/310457-spying-after-snowden-whats-changed-and-what-hasnt.

5 Donald Trump, quoted in Cynthia McFadden and William Arkin, "Russia Considers Returning Snowden to U.S. to 'Curry Favor' with Trump: Official," NBC News, February 11, 2017, http://www.nbcnews.com/news/us-news/russia-eyes-sending-snowden-u-s-gift-trump-official-n718921.

6 Juan Zarate, quoted in ibid.

Chapter 5

1 Arne Christian Haugstoyl, quoted in Agence France-Presse in Oslo, "Norway Accuses Group Linked to Russia of Carrying Out Cyber-Attack," *Guardian*, February 3, 2017, https://www.theguardian.com/technology/2017/feb/03/norway-accuses-group-linked-to-russia-of-carrying-out-cyber-attack.

2 Erna Solberg, quoted in Hyacinth Mascarenhas, "Norway Blames Russia-Linked Hackers for Cyberattack Targeting Spy Agency, Ministries," *International Business Times*, February 4, 2017, http://www.ibtimes.co.uk/norway-blames-russia-linked-hackers-cyberattack-targeting-spy-agency-ministries-1604809.

3 "Russian Hacking and the Baltic States," *Geopolitical Monitor*, March 28, 2017, https://www.geopoliticalmonitor.com/russian-hacking-and-the-baltic-states/.

4 Stephen Jewkes and Oleg Vukmanovic, "Russia-Backed Hackers Suspected in Cyber Attacks of Baltic Energy Networks," Reuters, May 12, 2017, *Insurance Journal*, http://www.insurancejournal.com/news/international/2017/05/12/450906.htm.

5 Stephen Jewkes and Oleg Vukmanovic, "Suspected Russia-Backed Hackers Target Baltic Energy Networks," Reuters, May 11, 2017, http://www.reuters.com/article/us-baltics-cyber-insight-idUSKBN1871W5.

6 Quoted in ibid.

7 A. J. Vicens, "Russian Hackers May Now Be Mucking with European Elections," *Mother Jones*, February 27, 2017, http://www.motherjones.com/politics/2017/02/what-russia-european-elections.

8 James Lewis, quoted in Morgan Chalfant, "Russian Interference Looms over European Elections," *Hill*, April 21, 2017, http://thehill.com/policy/cybersecurity/329754-russian-interference-looms-over-european-elections.

9 *Moscow Times*, quoted in Vicens, "Russian Hackers."

10 Sergei Shoigu, quoted in ibid.

11 *New York Times*, quoted in ibid.

12 Richard Ferrand, quoted in Russ Read, "Macron Was Anticipating a Clinton-Sized Email Debacle, So He Went on a 'Counter-Offensive,'" *Daily Caller*, May 8, 2017, http://dailycaller.com/2017/05/08/macron-was-

anticipating-a-clinton-sized-email-debacle-so-he-went-on-a-counter-offensive/.

13 Sheera Frenkel, "Here's the Latest Evidence That Russian Hackers Are Targeting Europe's Elections," *Buzzfeed*, April 24, 2017, https://www.buzzfeed.com/sheerafrenkel/heres-the-latest-evidence-that-russian-hackers-are?utm_term=.00XZ1QXVQ#.jsMpar3Mr.

14 David E. Sanger, Scott Shane, and Andrew E. Kramer, "Russians Charged with Treason Worked in Office Linked to Election Hacking," *New York Times*, January 27, 2017. https://www.nytimes.com/2017/01/27/world/europe/russia-hacking-us-election.html?_r=2.

Chapter 6

1 Curtis M. Scaparrotti, quoted in "Ukraine 'Almost Reached' Arms Supplies Agreement with US—Poroshenko," RT, June 26, 2017, https://www.rt.com/news/394057-ukraine-us-arms-poroshenko/.

2 Stability and Democracy for Ukraine Act, H.R. 5094, 114th Cong., 2nd Session (2016), http://docs.house.gov/billsthisweek/20160919/HR5094.pdf?utm_source=Viber&utm_medium=Chat&utm_campaign=Private.

3 Alexander Vershbow, "How Trump Can Fix US-Russia Ties," Atlantic Council, May 8, 2017, http://www.atlanticcouncil.org/blogs/ukrainealert/how-trump-can-fix-us-russia-ties.

4 Colin H. Kahl, Ilan Goldenberg, and Nicholas A. Heras, "A Strategy for Ending the Syrian Civil War," Center for a New American Security, June 7, 2017 https://www.cnas.org/publications/reports/a-strategy-for-ending-the-syrian-civil-war.

5 Ibid.

6 Caleb Larson, "Countering Russian Hybrid Warfare," Atlantic Expedition, January 5, 2017, http://atlantic-expedition.org/countering-russian-hybrid-warfare-capabilities-and-propaganda/.

7 Weitz, "Countering Russia's Hybrid Threats."

8 Ibid.

9 Dan Goure, "NATO vs. Russia: How to Counter the Hybrid Warfare Challenge," *National Interest*, July 7, 2016, http://nationalinterest.org/blog/the-buzz/nato-vs-russia-how-counter-the-hybrid-warfare-challenge-16874?page=show.

10 Bryan Bender, "The Secret U.S. Army That Targets Moscow," *POLITICO*, April 14, 2016, http://www.politico.com/magazine/story/2016/04/moscow-pentagon-us-secret-study-213811.

11 H. R. McMaster, quoted in ibid.

12 Jon Wolfsthal, "After Deployment: What? Russian Violations of the INF Treaty," Carnegie Endowment for International Peace, March 30, 2017, http://carnegieendowment.org/2017/03/30/after-deployment-what-russian-violations-of-inf-treaty-pub-68514.

13 Zachary Cohen and Ryan Browne, "4 Times in 4 Days: Russian Military Aircraft Fly Off U.S. Coast," CNN, April 21, 2017, http://www.cnn.com/2017/04/21/politics/russian-bombers-tensions-trump/index.html.

14 Michael Hayden, quoted in ibid.

Chapter 7

1 "Welcome to the New Oil Order," *Financial Times*, January 28, 2016, https://www.ft.com/content/63790fdc-c5ad-11e5-b3b1-7b2481276e45.

2 Anthony Fensom, "America Is Smashing Russia and OPEC's Grip on the Oil Market," *National Interest*, August 14, 2016, http://nationalinterest.org/feature/america-smashing-russia-opecs-grip-the-oil-market-17340.

3 Sergey Shmatko, quoted in ibid.

4 Ibid.

5 Srinivas Mazumdaru, "Western Sanctions and Languid Russian Economy," Deutsche Welle, February 5, 2017, http://www.dw.com/en/western-sanctions-and-languid-russian-economy/a-38668372.

6 Vladimir Putin, quoted in Kenneth Rapoza, "Putin Admits Sanctions Sapping Russia," *Forbes*, October 21, 2016, https://www.forbes.com/sites/kenrapoza/2016/10/21/putin-admits-sanctions-sapping-russia/print/.

Chapter 8

1 Kimberly Marten, "Reducing Tensions between Russia and NATO," Council on Foreign Relations, March 2017, http://www.cfr.org/nato/reducing-tensions-between-russia-nato/p38899.

2 Tom Batchelor, "The Map That Shows How Many NATO Troops Are Deployed along Russia's Border," *Independent*, February 5, 2017, http://www.independent.co.uk/news/world/europe/russia-nato-border-forces-map-where-are-they-positioned-a7562391.html.

3 Ibid.

4 Ibid.

5 Data Team, "Military Spending by NATO Members: Does America Contribute More Than Its Fair Share?," *Economist*, February 16, 2017, http://www.economist.com/blogs/graphicdetail/2017/02/daily-chart-11.

6 Marten, "Reducing Tensions."

7 Richard N. Haass, "Donald Trump: What the President Should Do about Russia," *TIME*, February 17, 2017, http://time.com/4675581/haass-russia-trump/.

8 Marten, "Reducing Tensions."

9 Ibid.

10 Haass, "Donald Trump."

11 Eugene Rumer, Richard Sokolsky, and Paul Stronksi, "U.S. Policy toward Central Asia 3.0," Carnegie Endowment for International Peace, January

25, 2016, http://carnegieendowment.org/2016/01/25/u.s.-policy-toward-central-asia-3.0-pub-62556.

12 Alexey Drobinin, quoted in Seth J. Frantzman, "Despite Syria, Israel-Russia Relations Are the Warmest in History," *Jerusalem Post*, March 25, 2017, http://www.jpost.com/Israel-News/Despite-Syria-Israel-Russia-relations-are-the-warmest-in-history-485062.

13 Benjamin Netanyahu, quoted in Avi Lewis, "Netanyahu on Iran Deal: The More You Read It, the Worse It Gets," *Times of Israel*, July 15, 2015, http://www.timesofisrael.com/netanyahu-on-iran-deal-the-more-you-read-it-the-worse-it-gets/.

14 Robert D. Blackwill and Philip H. Gordon, *Repairing the U.S.-Israel Relationship* (New York: Council on Foreign Relations Press, 2016), http://www.cfr.org/israel/repairing-us-israel-relationship/p38484.

15 Ilan Goldenberg and Julie Smith, "U.S.-Russia Competition in the Middle East Is Back," *Foreign Policy*, March 7, 2017, http://foreignpolicy.com/2017/03/07/u-s-russia-competition-in-the-middle-east-is-back/.

16 Curtis Scaparrotti, quoted in U.S.-Ukraine Business Council, *USUBC—Washington Watch—Report 19*, USUBC, April 4, 2017, http://www.usubc.org/site/USUBC-Washington-Watch/usubc---washington-watch---report-nbsp-19-nbsp-.

17 Eric Schmitt, "U.S. Troops Train in Eastern Europe to Echoes of the Cold War," *New York Times*, August 6, 2017, https://www.nytimes.com/2017/08/06/world/europe/russia-america-military-exercise-trump-putin.html?_r=2.

18 "U.S. Deploys Advanced Anti-Aircraft Missiles in Baltics for First Time," Reuters, July 10, 2017, https://www.reuters.com/article/us-usa-baltics-patriot/u-s-deploys-advanced-anti-aircraft-missiles-in-baltics-for-first-time-idUSKBN19V28A.

Chapter 9

1 Richard Shirreff, quoted in Evan Osnos, David Remnick, and Joshua Yaffa, "Trump, Putin, and the New Cold War," *New Yorker*, March 6, 2017, http://www.newyorker.com/magazine/2017/03/06/trump-putin-and-the-new-cold-war.

2 Strobe Talbott, quoted in Alison Smale and Andrew Higgins, "Putin and Merkel: A Rivalry of History, Distrust and Power," *New York Times*, March 12, 2017, https://www.nytimes.com/2017/03/12/world/europe/vladimir-putin-angela-merkel-russia-germany.html.

3 Angela Merkel, quoted in Giulia Paravicini, "Angela Merkel: Europe Must Take 'Our Fate' into Own Hands," *POLITICO*, May 28, 2017, http://www.politico.eu/article/angela-merkel-europe-cdu-must-take-its-fate-into-its-own-hands-elections-2017/.

4 Emmanuel Macron, quoted in Michel Rose and Denis Dyomkin, "After

Talks, France's Macron Hits Out at Russian Media, Putin Denies Hacking," Reuters, May 29, 2017, http://www.reuters.com/article/us-france-russia-idUSKBN18P030.

5 "Canada's Foreign Minister on Tillerson, the G-7 and Russia," interview with Chrystia Freeland, by Rachel Martin, *Morning Edition*, April 13, 2017, NPR, http://www.npr.org/2017/04/13/523725498/canadas-foreign-minister-on-tillerson-the-g7-and-russia.

6 Chrystia Freeland, quoted in "Allies Start Planning a Life without America," *New York Times*, June 17, 2017, https://www.nytimes.com/2017/06/17/opinion/sunday/allies-start-planning-a-life-without-america.html.

7 Malcolm Turnbull, quoted in Gabrielle Chan, "Malcolm Turnbull Tells Russia to Pull Bashar Al-Assad into Line after US Missile Strikes," *Guardian*, April 08, 2017, https://www.theguardian.com/australia-news/2017/apr/09/no-us-request-for-help-after-attack-on-assad-base-australian-defence-minister-says.

8 Malcolm Turnbull, quoted in ibid.

Chapter 10

1 John Dickson, quoted in Levi Maxey, "Disentangling the NSA and Cyber Command—the Cipher Brief," Cipher Brief, July 25, 2017, https://www.thecipherbrief.com/article/north-america/disentangling-nsa-and-cyber-command-1092.

2 John Dickson, quoted in ibid.

3 John McCain, quoted in Stew Magnuson, "Roles, Responsibilities of Cyber Command Debated," *National Defense*, February 8, 2017, http://www.nationaldefensemagazine.org/articles/2017/2/8/roles-responsibilities-of-cyber-command-debated.

4 John Hyten, quoted in Sean D. Carberry, "General: Cyber Command Needs New Platform before NSA Split," FCW, April 4, 2017, https://fcw.com/articles/2017/04/04/cybercom-split-carberry.aspx.

5 Barack Obama, quoted in Sarah Lee, "Obama Orders US Russian Resorts Closed, Calls Them 'Spy Nests,'" *TheBlaze*, December 30, 2016, http://www.theblaze.com/news/2016/12/30/obama-orders-u-s-russian-resorts-closed-calls-them-spy-nests/.

6 Nicki Softness, "How Should the U.S. Respond to a Russian Cyberattack?," *Yale Journal of International Affairs*, February 27, 2017, http://yalejournal.org/article_post/how-should-the-u-s-respond-to-a-russian-cyberattack/.

7 Darlene Storm, "Ways $460 Million Military Contract for Cyber Bombs Could Attack Targets," *Computerworld*, November 25, 2015, http://www.computerworld.com/article/3007465/cybercrime-hacking/ways-460-million-military-contract-for-cyber-bombs-could-attack-targets.html.

8 Greg Miller, "As Russia Reasserts Itself, U.S. Intelligence Agencies Focus Anew on the Kremlin," *Washington Post*, September 14, 2016, https://www.washingtonpost.com/world/national-security/as-russia-reasserts-itself-us-intelligence-agencies-focus-anew-on-the-kremlin/2016/09/14/cc212c62-78f0-11e6-ac8e-cf8e0dd91dc7_story.html?utm_term=.ad7d091a31fa.

9 Quoted in ibid.

10 Quoted in Ali Watkins, "Russia Escalates Spy Games after Years of U.S. Neglect," *POLITICO*, June 01, 2017, http://www.politico.com/story/2017/06/01/russia-spies-espionage-trump-239003.

11 Dustin Volz, "Expiring Spying Law Helped U.S. Conclude Russia Hacked Election: NSA Chief," Reuters, May 11, 2017, http://www.reuters.com/article/us-usa-cyber-nsa-idUSKBN1872K1.

12 Mike Rogers, quoted in ibid.